Classic Cards

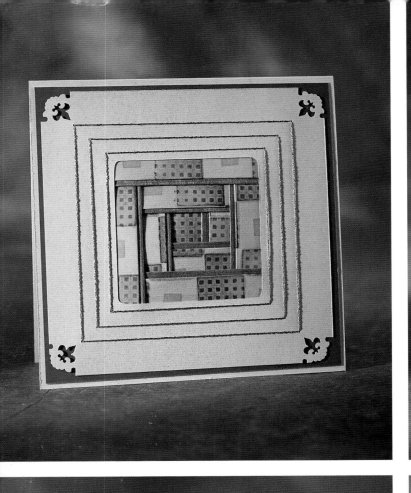
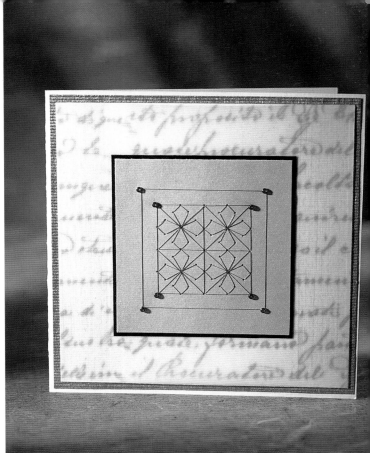

Classic Cards

60 Projects for the Discriminating Crafter

Marrian Piers

STERLING PUBLISHING CO., INC.

New York

Library of Congress Cataloging-in-Publication Data

Piers, Marrian.
  Classic cards : 60 projects for the discriminating crafter / Marrian Piers.
    p. cm.
  Includes bibliographical references and index.
  ISBN 1-4027-1072-0
  1. Greeting cards. 2. Handicraft. I. Title.

TT872.P54 2005
745.594'1--dc22

                                                                2005018823

10 9 8 7 6 5 4 3 2 1

Published in paperback in 2007 by Sterling Publishing Co., Inc.
387 Park Avenue South, New York, NY 10016
© 2005 by Marrian Piers
Distributed in Canada by Sterling Publishing
c/o Canadian Manda Group, 165 Dufferin Street
Toronto, Ontario, Canada M6K 3H6
Distributed in the United Kingdom by GMC Distribution Services
Castle Place, 166 High Street, Lewes, East Sussex, England BN7 1XU
Distributed in Australia by Capricorn Link (Australia) Pty. Ltd.
P.O. Box 704, Windsor, NSW 2756, Australia

Printed in China

Sterling ISBN-13: 978-1-4027-1072-8 Hardcover
        ISBN-10: 1-4027-1072-0
        ISBN-13: 978-1-4027-4739-7 Paperback
        ISBN-10: 1-4027-4739-X

For information about custom editions, special sales, or premium
and corporate purchases, please contact Sterling Special Sales
Department at 800-805-5489 or specialsales@sterlingpub.com.

This book is dedicated to my mother, Ann, whose constant encouragement and support have been a blessing in my life.

To my husband, Warren, and our three children, Jeff, Jared, and Rachel, thank you for all your patience and support during the writing of this book and for providing me with my own cheering section.

To Danielle Truscott at Sterling Publishing, thank you for your ongoing encouragement and direction throughout this project.

And finally, this book would never have come together without the wisdom and dedication to detail that my editor, Barbara Machtiger, provided. I will always appreciate your perseverance and friendship.

CONTENTS

INTRODUCTION

Making greeting cards is one of the most pleasurable pastimes for anyone who enjoys handmade crafts. There exists such a broad variety of materials and techniques to choose from in card making that one or more styles are bound to catch the eye of the craftsperson.

In this book we explore a branch of card making that originated in The Netherlands. The Dutch have long enjoyed making cards, ranking it among their favorite crafts. In recent years, several paper folding techniques, including teabag, iris, and kaleidoscope folding, as well as embroidery on cards, have made their way to North America. Many have enjoyed using these new techniques to create unique cards for any occasion, and still others have discovered the lovely cards resulting from these techniques, which range from simple stitched borders to elaborate three-dimensional motifs. These European card-making techniques are the foundation for the cards in this book.

Browse the chapters to discover the array of intriguing designs. Because so many of the cards incorporate embroidery, either as the primary embellishment or as just one part of the overall design, we begin there. Then we explore this basic style further by combining it with center medallions, teabag folding, iris folding, napkin cutouts, beads, and kaleidoscope cards.

The cards are arranged by degree of difficulty, each chapter beginning with the easiest and progressing to the more challenging. Clear, concise, simple-to-follow instructions, stitching patterns, and folding and construction diagrams will help to produce the beautiful results you see in a relatively short time. Once you're comfortable with the techniques, allow your imagination and creative spirit to lead you to design your own greeting cards.

Be sure to read the remainder of this introduction, which will acquaint you with the materials you'll need to make all the cards in this book as well as provide you with some basic information about the processes involved in their making.

A final note: Whether we are on the sending or receiving end of a handmade greeting card, the pleasure principle is the same. Through the simple task of putting a card together, we express our love and caring for the recipient, sentiments that are acknowledged as soon as the envelope is opened.

Materials You'll Need

The following is a general list of materials needed to make the cards in this book. Most of them can be readily found at crafts, art-supply, scrapbooking, stationery, fabric, and needlework/yarn stores. The Internet is another wonderful resource for all crafting supplies. And don't forget to check your own stash of crafts materials. You may already have papers and embellishments as well as some of the tools needed to make these projects.

Papers

CARDSTOCK. This is available in an array of colors, textures, and finishes, usually in 8½ x 11-inch sheets or 12-inch squares. The larger format will provide more paper and less waste when cutting it to size.

DECORATIVE AND PATTERNED PAPERS. These papers are useful as accent pieces and as decorative backgrounds. Some examples are gift-wrap, handmade, textured, marbled, and metallic-finish papers. Plain and patterned vellums are another good choice. Note that opaque vellums hide the adhesive better than the sheer kind.

ORIGAMI AND CHIYOGAMI PAPERS. Printed in beautiful, crisp colors and patterns, these Oriental papers can be folded and refolded many times without the ink wearing off the fold lines. They are good substitutes for teabag folding papers and add elegance to iris folding designs. The chiyogami papers are printed with designs taken from traditional fabrics used in making kimonos.

TEABAG FOLDING PAPERS. These 1½- or 2-inch paper squares with repeating designs come on individual sheets or in book form, both of which require the squares to be cut out. The books provide folding patterns as well as a selection of teabag papers.

PAPER NAPKINS. Paper napkins with patterns for every occasion and in any color are available at almost any food store, and in housewares, home décor, crafts, and party stores. Select soft, three-ply napkins.

ENVELOPES. The majority of the cards in this book will fit into 5 x 7-inch or 6-inch square envelopes. They can be found at general crafts, art-supply, and stationery stores.

Embellishments

THREADS. Threads come in every color and combination of colors (variegated) and in various thicknesses and finishes. Metallic threads are used extensively in projects throughout the book, but any type of thread, such as cotton, rayon, or embroidery floss, can be substituted. Threads are available in thicknesses ranging from cords or cables, which are very thin strands, to braids, which are several strands combined to give a thicker thread that will be more visible when stitched onto the cards.

RIBBONS. Ribbons are a great embellishment for cards. They can be used to add detail, such as a bow, or can substitute for the folded paper strips used in any of the iris folding projects. Choose ribbons that are either ⅜ inch or 9mm in width. Avoid very sheer ribbons, as the tape used in constructing the iris cards will show through.

SEED BEADS. Beads add dimension, color, and sparkle to greeting cards. Seed beads come in a variety of sizes and finishes. Look for size 11 seed beads with an iridescent luster or a glasslike, crystal, or metallic finish. Of course any bead can be substituted to suit personal preference.

FABRICS. Fabrics provide a richness and texture to cards that are different from paper. Any fabric, from a patterned brocade to a fine watercolor silk, can be used. When choosing a fairly lightweight fabric, iron fusible web to the wrong side as a stabilizer. This will give the fabric more body and make it easier to use. Select fusible web that has adhesive on one side only and follow the manufacturer's directions for application.

Tapes and Adhesives

TAPE. Removable tape is helpful for transferring patterns. Because it does not have a strong adhesive backing, it can be easily repositioned or removed without damaging the paper. Double-sided tape refers to tape that has adhesive on both sides. It is ideal for mounting the various layers onto the base card. Double-sided tape or thin, clear-drying glue can be used on opaque vellum. For many of the projects, particularly iris folding and kaleidoscope cards, common transparent tape is used to hold the strips and folded shapes in position. It is also used to secure the threads to the back of the work piece at the start and finish of stitching and when changing threads.

GLUE. Glue is necessary when making kaleidoscope or teabag folding cards. It can also be used as a substitute for double-sided tape. A good glue stick is recommended, as it does not dry immediately, allowing you to reposition pieces if necessary. Glue pens as well as white PVA (craft) glue can also be used, provided that they are not immediately tacky.

Tools and Accessories

SCISSORS. Most projects rely on the use of craft scissors for cutting paper and fabric. For a fancy edge use the decorative edging scissors found at general crafts, art-supply, and scrapbooking stores.

PAPER CUTTER OR PENCIL, CRAFT KNIFE, AND METAL RULER. To cut the required paper pieces for each project, a portable paper cutter, which has the ability to measure and cut at the same time, is a very useful tool. A good alternative is to measure and mark the paper with a ruler and pencil, then cut it to size with a craft knife.

SCORING TOOL AND PAPER FOLDER. Scoring blades are available as part of a paper cutter or are sold individually. An alternative is to position a ruler on the card where the fold should be, then using the ruler edge as a guide, gently mark a score line with a bone scorer, a craft knife, or a butter knife. To make crisp, neat folds on cardstock or paper, many people like to use the side of a bone paper folder. The tip of this tool can be used for scoring as well.

To achieve the same results, you can use your thumbnail or the dull side of a knife.

CUTTING MAT. This protective mat is made from resilient vinyl and comes in a number of sizes. It is often referred to as a "self-healing" mat because you can make numerous cuts into it without ruining it. Use it under paper when cutting with a craft knife or other sharp tool.

DECORATIVE EDGERS AND PUNCHES. These tools can add decorative edges or cutout corners to paper. They can be found in a wide assortment of small and large patterns. Scissor edgers are available for cutting decorative designs on either corners or edges, while craft punches punch out tiny shapes on any kind of paper.

PERFORATING TOOL. A perforating tool is necessary to make holes in cardstock in order to transfer the stitching pattern onto the card. Resembling a pen with a needle at one end, it is available in art supply and crafts stores and is sometimes referred to as a needle tool or piercing needle. Alternatives to this tool are a pin with a large head, such as a hat or corsage pin or a pushpin. A needle-point awl can also be used, but, like the pins, these will make a larger hole than desired. When stitching on a card that uses fine thread, a tiny hole is preferred to give the final project a professional look.

CRAFT FOAM PAD. Available in colorful 12 x 18-inch sheets 1/16–1/4 inch thick, craft foam provides a good surface on which to make perforations. The perforation tool must be able to pass through the pattern and the cardstock and into the foam to ensure a proper hole. The pad also prevents the tip of the perforating tool or pin from damage and your hands from getting sore. Use it on top of a cutting mat to provide added protection for your work surface. Layer two sheets of craft foam if one is too thin.

NEEDLES. The needles required for the projects in this book depend on the thickness of the embroidery threads and the holes of the beads used as embellishment. Generally you'll need a fine hand-sewing needle, an embroidery or crewel needle, and possibly a tapestry needle with a sharp point for use with the thicker braid threads. You'll also need a beading needle (either long and flexible or short and stiff). Have several of each variety on hand.

Getting Started

The following instructions offer general guidelines for using the patterns and techniques in *Classic Cards*. Details specific to each project and technique are explained in the appropriate chapter.

Transferring Embroidery Patterns

1. Select the card you'd like to make and photocopy the stitching pattern in black-and-white or color, as appropriate, onto 8½ x 11-inch paper.

2. To make the work piece, using a paper cutter or craft knife, metal ruler, and a cutting mat, cut a sheet of cardstock, in the color indicated for the project or the color of your choice, to the measurements provided.

3. Place the photocopied pattern over the front of the cardstock and hold it up to a light source (window or lamp). Position the cardstock so that the edges of the card are aligned with the outermost rules of the pattern. Maintaining this alignment, gently place the pattern and cardstock pattern side down onto the worktable and secure them in position with small pieces of removable tape placed on opposite edges of the back of the cardstock (photo 1). This will prevent the pattern and cardstock from shifting as the pattern is transferred. Turn the pattern / cardstock over so the pattern is facing up, and place them on a sheet of craft foam.

4. Using either a fine-point perforating tool or a straight pin, make a perforation everywhere a black dot appears on the pattern. Try to make each hole in the center of the dots so that the stitching will turn out neatly. Use a ruler as a guide when making perforations in a straight line. Be sure the point goes through the cardstock and into the foam (photo 2).

5. When all the perforations have been made, check the back of the cardstock for any places where you may have missed a dot. An easy way to do this is to hold the pattern up to the light. Any forgotten areas will show up quickly because light will shine through the perforations. Add any missed perforations. When complete, remove the tape from the back of the cardstock and lay the pattern aside. The perforated cardstock is now your work piece.

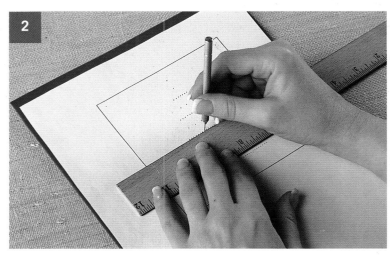

Transferring Iris Folding Patterns

The technique of iris folding involves placing folded strips of paper on a sequentially numbered pattern corresponding to a shape cut out of cardstock. The resulting design is in the form of an overlapping spiral that resembles the shutter of a camera or, as the term implies, the iris of an eye, as it closes.

1. If there is an embroidery pattern to be used with the card's iris folding pattern, follow steps 1–5 in Transferring Embroidery Patterns. If there is no stitching involved, follow steps 1 and 2 of Transferring Embroidery Patterns.

2. We've used Fiskars® ShapeCutter™ and ShapeTemplates™ system to cut the required shapes from the work piece to make a frame. Follow the manufacturer's instructions for use. If you want to use a stencil or template or other shape cutting system, see Before You Begin in chapter 4 for advice on adjusting patterns.

3. Once the work piece frame is cut out, place it wrong side up and centered over the corresponding pattern. This is particularly important when stitching has been done on the work piece. Place two small pieces of removable tape on opposite sides of the work piece to attach it to the pattern to prevent shifting. Then follow the individual project instructions.

Embroidering

To make the cards shown, use the cardstock and threads indicated for each project. If you are using cardstock of your own choosing, select a thread that compliments the design and color of each card. Unless otherwise noted, always use a single strand when stitching.

1. Cut a length of thread about 18 inches long. If thread is too long it may form knots or fray. When starting and ending a piece of thread, tape the end to the back of the cardstock instead of making a knot. Watch the tension of the thread as you pull it through. Keep the thread taut but not tight. If it is too tight it will cause the card to bend or pull to one side; if it is too loose, the stitching will look sloppy (photo 3).

2. Stitch the pattern as directed. To keep the back of the card as neat as possible and, at the same time, conserve thread, try going into the next closest hole as you sew (photo 4).

Adding Beads

If a pattern calls for beads to be sewn on, use a fine beading needle. Tape the end of the thread to the back of the card. Come up with needle and thread in the designated hole that requires a bead. Slip a bead onto the needle, then insert the needle back into the same hole, making sure the thread goes around the outside of the bead. Pull the thread through until it is taut, to ensure the bead will stay in place. If there are several beads to sew on, continue in this manner with the same piece of thread, moving from hole to hole until the project is completed. Trim the remaining thread and tape the end to the back of the card (photo 5).

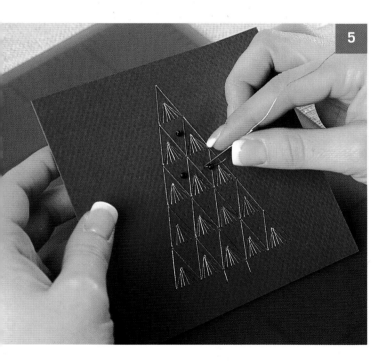

Teabag Folding

For this paper folding technique, 1½- and 2-inch squares of patterned paper are folded into identical shapes using various origami folds. The shapes, along with embroidery, form the design for the cards. Teabag folding papers come on sheets of squares, so

you can cut off the amount needed. Origami or chiyogami papers, which can also be used for this technique, must be measured before cutting. Imported teabag, origami, and chiyogami papers are printed using special inks that allow many folds without the printed design breaking down.

1. Make sure the squares are precisely cut to the measurements required for each project. Most projects require eight squares.

2. When using teabag papers with a distinct printed design, see that all papers are facing in the same direction before folding. This ensures that the same portion of the design will be showing on all the folded shapes.

3. Fold the teabag papers following the instructions and the folding illustrations provided for each project.

4. Use a glue stick to attach individual folded shapes to the work piece. Glue together individual folded papers that nest into each other to form a circle, then glue the circle to the work piece.

Kaleidoscope Folding

To make these cards, papers are folded into one of three shapes: strips folded in half, similar to those used in iris folding; triangles folded into squares; and triangles folded into kite shapes.

1. Fold the required numbers of strips, squares, or kites for each project.

2. Cut out the shape that will frame the kaleidoscope from cardstock.

3. Glue the folded papers to the work piece in the sequence shown on the pattern.

4. Do all embroidery before attaching the frame to the completed kaleidoscope design.

Mounting the Finished Work to the Card

When the work piece is completed, place double-sided tape on all edges on the wrong side of the piece. Generally, the work piece is centered over cardstock in a complimentary color cut to the slightly larger size indicated and mounted by pressing it in place. Depending on the project, however, you may be asked to position the work piece elsewhere on the cardstock. The mounted work piece may be mounted to a second and third piece of cardstock of graduated sizes. When the required number of layers have been added as background, the work has to be affixed to a scored and folded piece of cardstock, referred to as the base card (photo 6).

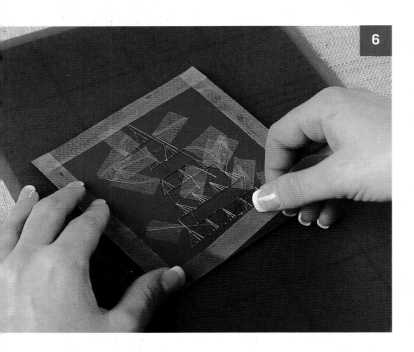

Scoring and Folding the Base Card

Cut the cardstock for the base card to the size indicated. Use a ruler and pencil to measure and mark the center of the base card. Make a score line across the center line with a scoring tool, the point of a bone paper folder, or the edge of a butter knife. Fold the card in half along the score line and make a sharp crease using a bone paper folder, butter knife, or your thumbnail (photo 7).

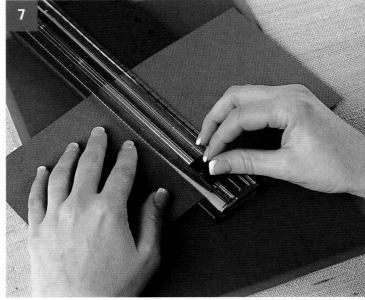

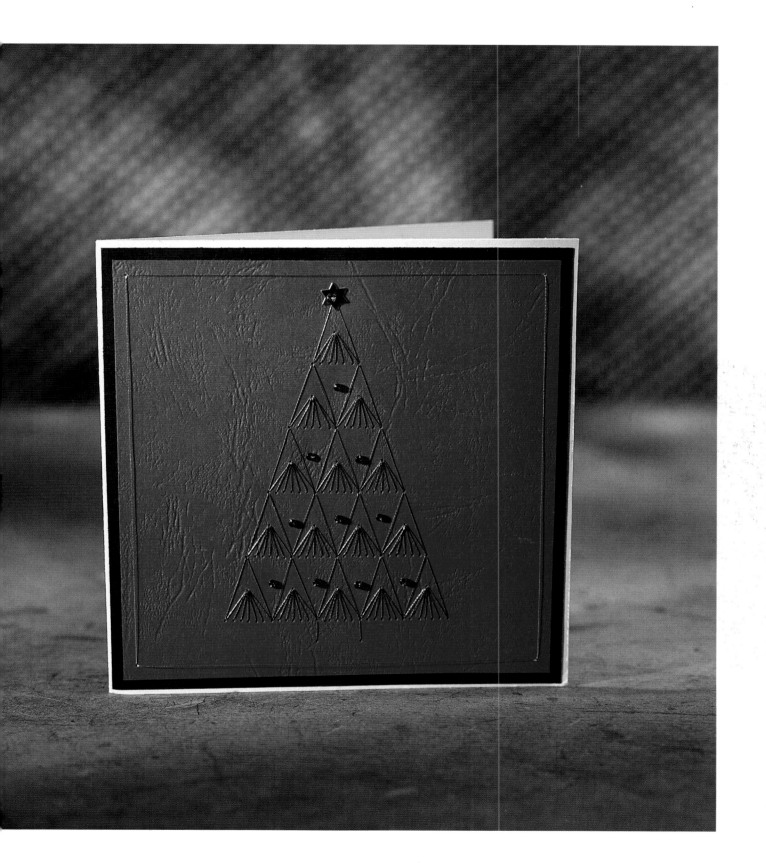

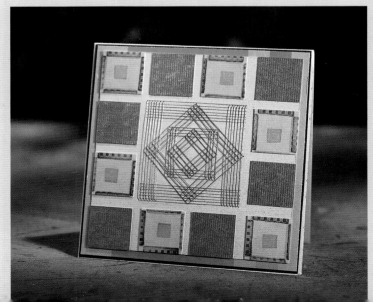

1

Embroidery

BEFORE YOU BEGIN

Many of the greeting cards in this book incorporate embroidery into their designs or feature it as the sole embellishment, so it is appropriate that the first decorating technique we take on is this popular needlecraft.

The embroidery patterns in this chapter and throughout utilize one simple embroidery stitch—the straight stitch. As its name implies, you stitch in a straight line from point to point. Long or short or any length between, the straight stitch is extremely versatile. It can be used to create borders, as in Geometric Star (page 32); to provide details, such as on the Chinese Pagodas card (page 20); and to form a variety of designs, such as the Christmas Tree (page 24) and Layered Squares (page 30).

Another type of embroidery pattern you'll encounter forms intricate-looking overlapping three-dimensional designs that resemble the "string art" images we made as children. The Circle Star (page 36) and Butterfly (page 38) are examples of this stitch-by-numbers technique. Although the resulting motifs appear complex, they are easily created by stitching in the numerical sequences provided.

Any embroidered design can be enhanced with other decorative elements, such as beads, buttons, and bits and pieces of decorative papers. You can also plan an embroidery design to include a cutout frame that will add depth and definition to the embroidery, as was done with the Holiday Ornament and Hearts cards (pages 28 and 34).

Read the sections on transferring the patterns and embroidering in Getting Started before you begin. Work with lengths of thread about 18 inches long, and instead of knotting the ends of the thread, tape them to the back of the work piece at the start and finish of stitching. As you embroider, keep your stitches taut to ensure the finished design looks sharp and neat.

Chinese Pagodas

This simple-to-make card incorporates scraps of decorative paper and large beads with embroidery to create a sophisticated collage of Asian-inspired elements.

PAPERS

Cardstock: black, ivory (8½ x 11-inch sheets); small pieces of metallic green and sage green

Decorative paper with a leaf design

Green/gold glossy marbled paper

EMBELLISHMENTS

Three flat beads or buttons with Asian motifs or three Chinese coins (1 inch in diameter)

Gold metallic thread #4 braid

SUPPLIES

Hand-sewing needle

Removable tape

Double-sided tape

Clear-drying craft glue

Scissors

Pencil

Paper cutter or craft knife and metal ruler

Craft foam (12 x 18-inch sheet)

Perforating tool

Scoring tool and bone paper folder (optional)

1. **CUT THE PAPERS:** From the black cardstock, cut a 5-inch square. From the ivory cardstock, cut a rectangle 5¼ x 10½ inches for the base card. From the metallic green cardstock, cut a rectangle 2 x 4 inches for the work piece. From the sage green cardstock, cut a rectangle 2¼ x 4¼ inches. From the leaf-design paper cut a rectangle 3½ x 1½ inches. From the marbled paper, cut three ¼ x 4-inch strips.

2. Score and fold the ivory base card (page 16) in half to form a 5¼-inch square.

3. Following the instructions in Getting Started (page 13), transfer the embroidery pattern for the pagodas to the metallic green work piece.

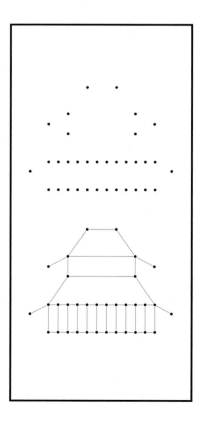

4. **EMBROIDER THE PATTERN:** With the pattern markings to guide you, stitch the pagodas using the gold metallic thread. It's easiest to stitch the vertical lines on the bottom of the pagoda first and then complete the outline stitches. Wrap the metallic thread twice around the top left corner of the work piece, pull taut, and tape to back.

5. **COMPLETE THE WORK PIECE:** Center and mount the completed work piece (page 16) onto the sage green rectangle using double-sided tape.

6. Tear along one long side of the leaf-design paper to make a deckle edge. Using double-sided tape, affix the torn paper to the left side of the black square, about 1 inch from the bottom edge (see photograph).

7. Align the layered work piece with the top edge of the leaf-design paper and mount it about ½ inch in from the deckle edge using double-sided tape.

8. Glue the flat beads, buttons, or coins onto the black square along the right side of the work piece.

9. Using the photo as a guide, glue the three marbled strips onto the far right of the black square as shown. Using the gold metallic thread, stitch the joints of the bamboo and the leaves as shown in the photo.

10. To finish, center and mount (page 16) all layers onto the front of the base card using double-sided tape.

TIP
Torn pieces of interesting paper, beads, stamping, and bits of natural materials such as shells, twigs, dried flowers, and grasses are creative embellishments for a card that uses a simple embroidery pattern.

Layered Triangles

The lovely patterns of chiyogami paper, which replicate those used on kimono fabrics, are a beautiful background against which to set a simple embroidery pattern. Here the delicate embroidery resembles the ribs of the leaves in the patterned paper.

YOU'LL NEED

PAPERS

Cardstock: black, white (8½ x 11-inch sheets)

Chiyogami or other decorative paper with gold-and-silver leaf design

EMBELLISHMENT

Gold metallic thread

SUPPLIES

Hand-sewing needle

Templates for 1- and 3-inch hexagons and cutting tool

Glue stick

Removable tape

Double-sided tape

Scissors

Pencil

Paper cutter or craft knife and metal ruler

Craft foam (12 x 18-inch square)

Perforating tool

Scoring tool and bone paper folder (optional)

1. **CUT THE PAPERS:** From the black cardstock cut a 3-inch square for the work piece and a 4¼-inch square. From the white cardstock cut a rectangle 5¼ x 10½ inches for the base card. From the chiyogami or other decorative paper, cut a 4-inch square and, using the template, cut a 1-inch hexagon.

2. Score and fold the white base card (page 16) in half to form a 5¼-inch square.

3. Following the instructions in Getting Started (page 13), transfer the embroidery pattern to the black work piece, making the necessary perforations.

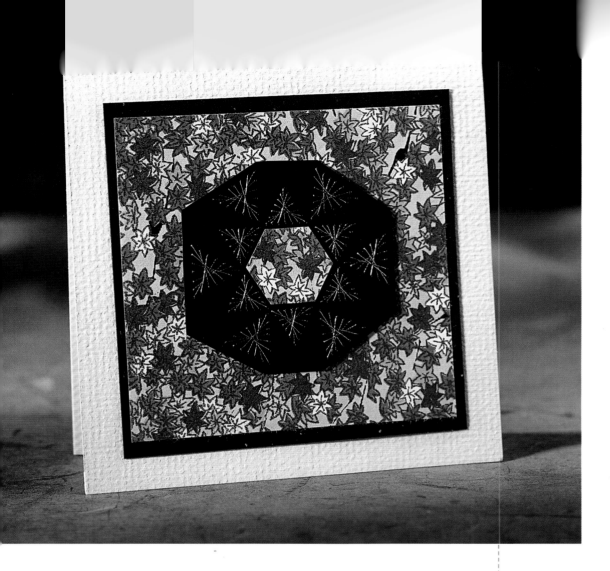

4. **EMBROIDER THE PATTERN:** With the pattern markings to guide you, stitch the large outer triangles using the gold metallic thread. Come out at hole 1 and go into hole 10. Continue stitching each triangle in a clockwise direction as follows: 11 – 2, 3 – 12, 13 – 4, 5 – 14, 15 – 6, 7 – 16, 17 – 8, 9 – 18. Stitch the smaller triangles in the same manner.

5. **COMPLETE THE WORK PIECE:** Glue the chiyogami hexagon in the center of the stitching on the work piece. Center the 3-inch hexagon template over the completed stitching, outline the shape, and cut it out. Alternatively, cut off equal sections from the four corners of the work piece. Or, if desired, leave the work piece intact.

6. Center and mount the completed work piece (page 16) onto the chiyogami square using double-sided tape. Similarly mount these layers onto the black square. To finish, center and mount all layers onto the front of the base card.

Christmas Tree

Decked out in traditional holiday colors, this festive tree design features embroidered branches and seed bead "ornaments." This is one Christmas card that's a definite keeper.

YOU'LL NEED

PAPERS

Cardstock: red, black, ivory
 (8½ x 11-inch sheets)

EMBELLISHMENTS

Green metallic thread

Gold metallic thread

Green seed beads (11)

Gold star sequin

SUPPLIES

Hand-sewing and beading
 needles

Removable tape

Double-sided tape

Scissors

Pencil

Paper cutter or craft knife and
 metal ruler

Perforating tool

Craft foam (12 x 18-inch sheet)

Scoring tool and bone paper
 folder (optional)

1. **CUT THE CARDSTOCK:** From the red, cut a 5-inch square for the work piece. From the black, cut a 5¼-inch square. From the ivory, cut a rectangle 5½ x 11 inches for the base card.

2. Score and fold the ivory base card (page 16) in half to form a 5½-inch square.

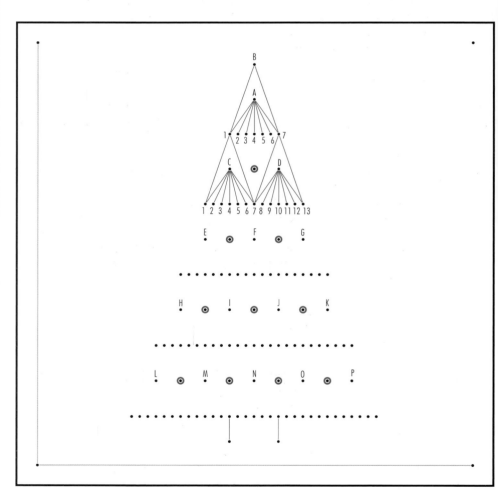

◉ bead

3. Following the instructions in Getting Started (page 13), transfer the embroidery pattern to the red work piece, making the necessary perforations.

4. **EMBROIDER THE PATTERN:** With the pattern markings to guide you, stitch the triangles that make up the tree. Each triangle is seven holes wide at the base. Each small, interior, triangle shares the same base with the larger triangle that surrounds it. Using green metallic thread, and working from the top triangle down, come out at hole A and go into holes 1–7, always returning to A to begin each new stitch. Outline the first triangle by coming out at hole B and going into holes 1 and 7 only.

5. Stitch the second row of triangles: Come out at hole C and go into holes 1–7 as in step 4, then come out at hole D and go into holes 7–13 in the same manner. Outline each of these triangles as shown. Continue stitching each row of triangles in the same manner, then add the two straight stitches for the trunk.

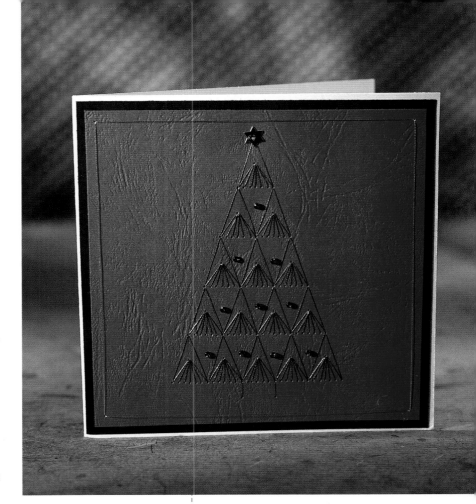

6. **SEW ON BEADS:** Following the instructions for adding beads (page 15), and using the pattern markings and photograph as guides, sew a bead in the center of each inverted triangle. Sew the star sequin and the remaining bead to hole B at the top of the tree.

7. **COMPLETE THE STITCHING:** Using the gold metallic thread, stitch from corner to corner to make the border.

8. Center and mount the completed work piece (page 16) onto the black square using double-sided tape. To finish, center and mount these layers onto the front of the base card in the same manner.

VARIATION

Perforate the top three triangles on the pattern to make a small Christmas tree for a gift card, or make two small trees, one above the other, to decorate another version of the featured card as shown. Add long stitches at left and right sides as borders.

Floral Design

The floral pattern, done in straight stitches of varying lengths, evokes the words of an old nursery rhyme: "with silver bells and cockle shells and pretty maids all in a row."

YOU'LL NEED

PAPERS

Cardstock: white, plum, sage green (8½ x 11-inch sheets)

Decorative papers: lightweight green, metallic mauve (8½ x 11-inch sheets)

EMBELLISHMENTS

Mauve metallic thread #4 braid

Variegated gold/green/purple metallic thread #4 braid

Gold metallic thread

SUPPLIES

Hand-sewing needle

Removable tape

Double-sided tape

Scissors

Pencil

Paper cutter or craft knife and metal ruler

Craft foam (12 x 18-inch sheet)

Perforating tool

Scoring tool and bone paper folder (optional)

1. **CUT THE PAPERS:** From the white cardstock, cut a 4½-inch square for the work piece. From the plum cardstock, cut a 5-inch square. From the sage green cardstock, cut a rectangle 5¼ x 10½ inches for the base card. From the lightweight green paper, cut a 4¼-inch square. From the metallic mauve paper, cut a 4¾-inch square.

2. Score and fold the sage green base card (page 16) in half to form a 5½-inch square.

3. **PREPARE THE WORK PIECE:** Center and mount the lightweight green square onto the white square using double-sided tape. Together they form the work piece.

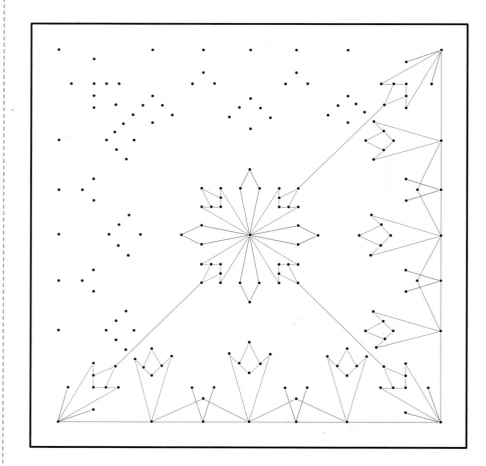

4. Following the instructions in Getting Started (page 13), transfer the embroidery pattern to the work piece, making the necessary perforations.

5. **EMBROIDER THE PATTERN:** With the pattern markings for side A to guide you, and using the mauve metallic thread, stitch the flowers on each side of the card and in the center as shown. Next, stitch the leaves using the variegated gold/green/purple thread. Using the gold metallic thread, stitch the outer borders, center cross, and angled lines connecting the leaves and flowers.

6. Center and mount the completed work piece (page 16) onto the metallic mauve square using double-sided tape. Similarly mount these layers onto the plum square. To finish, center and mount all layers onto the front of the base card.

TIP
If you find a beautiful piece of paper that is too thin to use as the work piece, cut a piece of cardstock, in a matching or complementary color, about ¼ inch larger than the work piece and glue the paper to the cardstock. This will make the thin paper sturdy enough to perforate and stitch.

Holiday Ornament

Straight stitches are used in a number of ways to create this delightful holiday ornament card. Three different types of glittery threads and a few twinkling beads add festive flare.

YOU'LL NEED

PAPERS

Cardstock: gold pearl, olive green pearl, dark purple, white sparkle (8½ x 11-inch sheets)

EMBELLISHMENTS

Gold metallic thread

Copper metallic thread #4 braid

Variegated gold/green/purple metallic thread #4 braid

Green seed beads (5)

SUPPLIES

Template for 3-inch circle and cutting tool

Corner punch

Hand-sewing and beading needles

Removable tape

Double-sided tape

Scissors

Pencil

Paper cutter or craft knife and metal ruler

Craft foam (12 x 18-inch sheet)

Perforating tool

Scoring tool and bone paper folder (optional)

1. **CUT THE CARDSTOCK:** From the gold pearl, cut a 4-inch square for the work piece. From the olive green, cut a 5-inch square. From the dark purple, cut a 5¼-inch square. From the white sparkle, cut a rectangle 5½ x 11 inches for the base card.

2. Score and fold the white sparkle base card (page 16) in half to form a 5½-inch square.

3. Following the instructions in Getting Started (page 13), transfer the embroidery pattern to the gold work piece, making the necessary perforations.

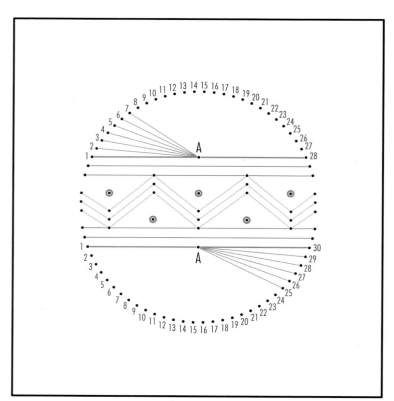

⊚ bead

4. **EMBROIDER THE PATTERN:** With the marked pattern to guide you, stitch the top and bottom of the ornament using the gold metallic thread. Come out at hole A at the top and go into holes 1–28, always returning to A to start each stitch. Stitch the bottom of the ornament in the same manner, except stitch into holes 1–30.

5. Using the copper metallic thread, stitch the center chevron design. Using the variegated thread, stitch the three dividing lines on the top and bottom of the ornament as shown.

6. **SEW ON BEADS:** Following the instructions for adding beads (page 15), sew the green beads between the chevrons as shown, using the gold metallic thread.

7. **MAKE THE BOW:** Using a double strand of the copper metallic thread, fashion a simple bow; trim the ends. Using the gold metallic thread, stitch the bow to the top of the ornament through two perforations, taping the ends of the thread to the back of the work piece.

8. Using the template, draw a 3-inch-diameter circle in the center of the wrong side of the olive green square and cut out. Turn the cutout square right side up. Center the completed work piece behind the opening and secure it with double-sided tape. Use a corner punch to decoratively cut the four corners of the framed work piece.

9. Center and mount the work piece (page 16) onto the dark purple square using double-sided tape. To finish, center and mount these layers onto the front of the base card in the same manner.

Layered Squares

This eye-popping design, with its graduated overlapping stitched squares in alternating colors and the complementary paper-square border, is sure to brighten anyone's day, whether you're sending a birthday greeting, a thank-you note, or get-well wishes.

YOU'LL NEED

PAPERS

Cardstock: lime green, forest green, ivory (8½ x 11-inch sheets)

Decorative paper with green design (8½ x 11-inch sheet)

Metallic lime green paper (8½ x 11-inch sheet)

Decorative paper with green-patterned squares (8½ x 11-inch sheet)

EMBELLISHMENTS

Lime green metallic thread

Gold metallic thread

SUPPLIES

Hand-sewing needle

Removable tape

Double-sided tape

Glue stick

Scissors

Pencil

Paper cutter or craft knife and metal ruler

Craft foam (12 x 18-inch sheet)

Perforating tool

Scoring tool and bone paper folder (optional)

1. **CUT THE PAPERS:** From the lime green cardstock, cut a 4¾-inch square for the work piece. From the forest green cardstock, cut a 5¼-inch square. From the ivory cardstock, cut a rectangle 5½ x 11 inches for the base card. From the green-design paper, cut a 5-inch square. From the metallic lime green and square-patterned papers, cut six 1-inch squares each.

2. Score and fold the ivory base card (page 16) in half to form a 5½-inch square.

3. Following the instructions in Getting Started (page 13), transfer the embroidery pattern to the lime green work piece, making the necessary perforations.

4. **EMBROIDER THE PATTERN:** With the pattern markings to guide you, stitch the graduated squares, from smallest to largest. Stitch two opposite sides of each square first, then stitch the remaining sides, always working from the inside outward. Keep the threads taut but not tight to prevent them from pulling to one side. Using the lime green thread, stitch the center square: Come out at hole 1 and go into hole 2. From there go from 3 – 4, 5 – 6, 7 – 8. Follow this sequence on the opposite side. Stitch the two remaining sides in the same manner.

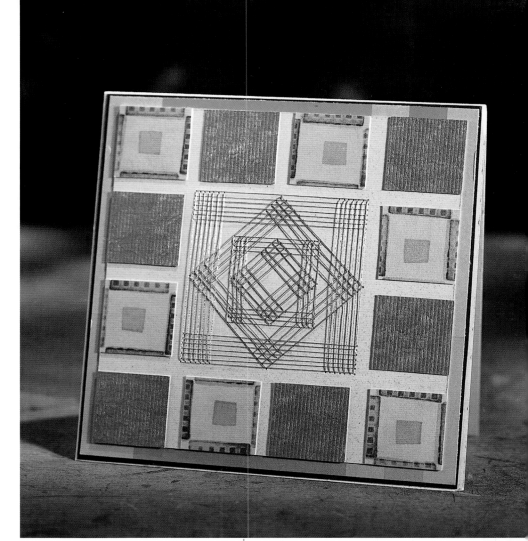

5. Alternating between green and gold threads, stitch the next three overlapping squares as you did the first square, following the numerical sequence.

6. Glue the 1-inch squares along the sides of the work piece, alternating between the two papers.

7. Center and mount the completed work piece (page 16) onto the square of paper with green designs using double-sided tape. Similarly mount these layers onto the forest green square. To finish, center and mount all layers onto the front of the base card.

VARIATION

Make this gift card by stitching only the two smallest squares onto a 2-inch work piece. Use a heavier metallic thread for the smaller of the two colored squares. When complete, cut a frame to fit the work piece from the center of a 3-inch square of patterned coordinating paper. Center and mount the work piece to the back of the frame and mount both to a 3¼-inch square of cardstock. Finish by mounting all layers to a scored and folded 3½ x 7-inch base card.

Geometric Star

Using several types and weights of metallic thread to make a variety of straight-stitching designs adds dimension and results in an elegant card with clean, modern lines.

YOU'LL NEED

PAPERS

Cardstock: navy blue, light blue (8½ x 11-inch sheets), white sparkle (12 x 12-inch sheet)

EMBELLISHMENTS

Silver/black twist metallic thread

Light blue metallic thread #4 braid

Silver cable metallic thread

Clear seed beads (4)

SUPPLIES

Sewing and beading needles

Removable tape

Double-sided tape

Scissors

Pencil

Paper cutter or craft knife and metal ruler

Craft foam (12 x 18-inch sheet)

Perforating tool

Scoring tool and bone paper folder (optional)

1. **CUT THE CARDSTOCK:** From the navy, cut a 4½-inch square for the work piece and a 5½-inch square. From the light blue, cut a 5¼-inch square. From the white sparkle, cut a rectangle 5¾ x 11½ inches for the base card.

2. Score and fold the white sparkle base card (page 16) in half to form a 5¾-inch square.

3. Following the instructions in Getting Started (page 13), transfer the embroidery pattern to the navy work piece, making the necessary perforations.

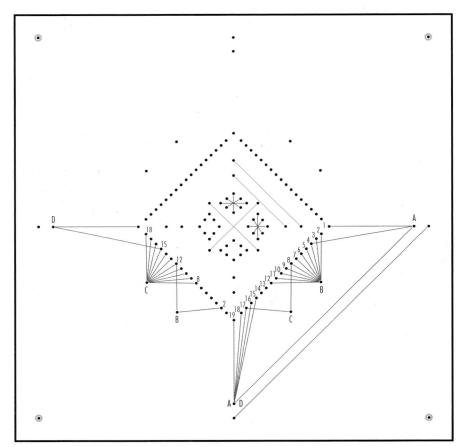

⊙ **bead**

4. **EMBROIDER THE PATTERN:** With the pattern markings to guide you, stitch the large star: Using the silver/black twist metallic thread, come out at hole A and go into holes 1–5, always returning to A to start each new stitch. Then move to hole B and stitch from there to holes 2–12 in the same manner. Continue stitching in this manner from hole C to holes 8–18 and from hole D to holes 15–19. Repeat to stitch each side of the star.

5. After completing the large star, use the light blue metallic braid to stitch the four center stars as shown. Be sure the stitches are done in the same order for each of the four stars.

6. Using the silver cable metallic thread, stitch the square borders surrounding the center stars. Use the light blue metallic braid to stitch the borders surrounding the large star.

7. **SEW ON BEADS:** Following the instructions for adding beads (page 15) and using the silver/black twist metallic thread and beading needle, sew one seed bead to each corner of the work piece where indicated.

8. Center and mount the completed work piece (page 16) onto the light blue square using double-sided tape. Similarly center and mount these layers onto the remaining navy square. To finish, center and mount all layers onto the front of the base card.

Hearts

There is no symbol of love and caring more universal than the heart. Here two concentric hearts are straight-stitched using the stitch-by-numbers technique to create a string art design. More hearts are found in the border of beads and the cutout window that frames them all.

YOU'LL NEED

PAPERS

Cardstock: metallic light blue, metallic gray/black swirl, black, mottled silver/black (8½ x 11-inch sheets)

EMBELLISHMENTS

Silver/blue metallic twist thread

Gold/silver metallic thread #4 braid

Blue seed beads (34)

SUPPLIES

Hand-sewing and beading needles

Fiskars® ShapeCutter™ and Hearts ShapeTemplate™ or template for 3½-inch heart and cutting tool

Removable tape

Double-sided tape

Scissors

Pencil

Paper cutter or craft knife and metal ruler

Craft foam (12 x 18-inch sheet)

Perforating tool

Scoring tool and bone paper folder (optional)

1. **CUT THE CARDSTOCK:** From the metallic light blue, cut a 4-inch square for the work piece. From the metallic black/gray swirl, cut a 5-inch square. From the black, cut a 5⅛-inch square. From the mottled silver/black, cut a rectangle 5¼ x 10½ inches for the base card.

2. Score and fold the mottled silver/black base card (page 16) in half to form a 5¼-inch square.

3. Following the instructions in Getting Started (page 13), transfer the embroidery pattern to the metallic light blue work piece, making the necessary perforations.

◎ **bead**

4. **EMBROIDER THE PATTERN:** With the pattern markings to guide you, stitch the small center heart using the silver/blue metallic thread. Come out at hole 1 and go into hole 13. Continue stitching in the following sequence: 14 – 2, 3 – 15, 16 – 4, 5 – 17, 18 – 6, 7 – 19, 20 – 8, 9 – 21, 22 – 10, 11 – 23, 24 – 12.

5. Using the gold/silver thread, stitch the right side of the large heart: Come out at hole 1 and go into hole 18. Continue stitching in the following sequence: 19 – 2, 3 – 20, 21 – 4, 5 – 22, 23 – 6, 7 – 24, 25 – 8, 9 – 26, 27 – 10, 11 – 28, 29 – 12, 13 – 30, 31 – 14, 15 – 32, 33 – 16, 17 – 34, 35 – 18. Beginning at hole 1 again, stitch the left side of the heart in the same manner.

6. **SEW ON BEADS:** Following the instructions for adding beads (page 15), and using the gold/silver thread and beading needle, stitch a blue bead to every other perforation outlining the heart, as shown in the photograph.

7. **COMPLETE THE WORK PIECE:** Using the ShapeCutter™ and the 3½-inch heart from the template, cut out the heart shape from the metallic black/gray square. If using a separate heart template and cutting tool, outline the heart onto the center of the wrong side of the metallic black/gray square and cut out. Turn the cutout square right side up. Center the stitched work piece behind the heart-shaped opening and secure it with double-sided tape. (As an alternative, the square work piece can be mounted directly onto the uncut metallic black/gray square.)

8. Center and mount the framed work piece (page 16) onto the black square using double-sided tape. To finish, center and mount all layers onto the front of the base card.

VARIATION

Stitch the small heart onto one quadrant of a square of cardstock. Then, from pretty vellum cut to the same size as the work piece, cut out a square or circle to make a frame for the heart and mount it to the cardstock. Finish the card by mounting it onto layers of complementary or matching papers. This card can be made much smaller to use as a gift tag.

Circle Star

This stitch-by-numbers design is reminiscent of the "string art" images we enjoyed making as children. Only a circle of perforations and straight stitches done in a precise numerical sequence are needed to make this complex-looking pattern.

YOU'LL NEED

PAPERS

Cardstock: dark purple, black pearl, white sparkle (8½ x 11-inch sheets)

Metallic mauve paper (8½ x 11-inch sheet)

EMBELLISHMENTS

Lavender metallic thread #4 braid

Variegated green/gold/black metallic thread #4 braid

SUPPLIES

Hand-sewing needle

Template for 3-inch circle and cutting tool

Corner punch

Removable tape

Double-sided tape

Glue stick

Scissors

Pencil

Paper cutter or craft knife and metal ruler

Craft foam (12 x 18-inch sheet)

Perforating tool

Scoring tool and bone paper folder (optional)

1. **CUT THE PAPERS:** From the dark purple cardstock cut a 3½-inch square for the work piece. From the black pearl cardstock cut a 4¾-inch square. From the white sparkle cardstock cut a rectangle 5¼ x 10½ inches for the base card. From the metallic mauve paper cut a 5-inch square.

2. Score and fold the white sparkle base card (page 16) in half to form a 5¼-inch square.

3. Following the instructions in Getting Started (page 13), transfer the embroidery pattern to the purple work piece, making the necessary perforations.

4. **EMBROIDER THE PATTERN:** With the pattern markings to guide you, stitch the stars, carefully following the sequence of numbers below. You'll notice that the stitches for the first star are spaced eleven holes apart; the second star, eight holes apart. Using the lavender metallic thread, stitch the first star: Come out at hole 1

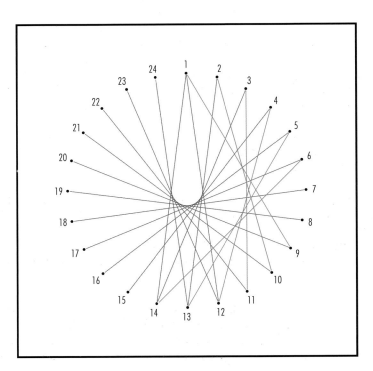

and go into hole 12. Continue stitching in the following sequence:
13 – 2, 3 – 14, 15 – 4, 5 – 16, 17 – 6, 7 – 18, 19 – 8, 9 – 20, 21 – 10,
11 – 22, 23 – 12, 13 – 24, 1 – 14, 15 – 2, 3 – 16, 17 – 4, 5 – 18, 19 – 6,
7 – 20, 21 – 8, 9 – 22, 23 – 10, 11 – 24. The bottom star is completed when each hole has two lavender stitches coming out.

5. Use the variegated thread to stitch the second, overlapping, star:
Come out at hole 1 and go into hole 9. Continue stitching in the
following sequence: 10 – 2, 3 – 11, 12 – 4, 5 – 13, 14 – 6, 7 – 15, 16
– 8, 9 – 17, 18 – 10, 11 – 19, 20 – 12, 13 – 21, 22 – 14, 15 – 23, 24 –
16, 17 – 1, 2 – 18, 19 – 3, 4 – 20, 21 – 5, 6 – 22, 23 – 7, 8 – 24. The
overlapping star is completed when each hole has two variegated
stitches coming out.

6. Using the template, draw a 3-inch-diameter circle in the center of
the wrong side of the black pearl square and cut out. Turn the cutout square right side up. Center the completed work piece behind
the opening and secure it with double-sided tape. Use a corner
punch to decoratively cut the four corners of the framed work
piece, saving two of the cut corners.

7. Center and mount the framed work piece (page 16) onto the
mauve metallic square using double-sided tape. Glue the two saved
corners to two diagonally opposing corners of the square. To
finish, center and mount all layers onto the front of the base card.

TIP
When using the straight stitch to
create a string art design, the
amount of spaces between
stitches alters the look of the
finished product. For example,
the center of the Circle Star will
be larger if fewer holes are
skipped between sitiches (skip
six holes between stitches as
opposed to nine).

VARIATION
*Using fine metallic threads in black and
gold on red sparkle paper would make
this card appropriate for Christmas.*

Butterfly

Worked in bold colors and two weights of threads, the three-dimensional butterfly is done in straight stitches following the numerical sequences on the pattern. The result looks intricate but is actually easy to create.

YOU'LL NEED

PAPERS

Cardstock: ivory pearl, ivory
(8½ x 11-inch sheets)

Decorative paper in a mottled
green/brown/ivory design
(8½ x 11-inch sheet)

Textured metallic gold/silver paper
(8½ x 11-inch sheet)

EMBELLISHMENTS

Gold metallic thread

Variegated green/gold/black
metallic thread #4 braid

Gold metallic thread #4 braid

SUPPLIES

Hand-sewing needle

Removable tape

Double-sided tape

Paper cutter or craft knife and
metal ruler

Scissors

Pencil

Craft foam (12 x 18-inch sheet)

Perforating tool

Scoring tool and bone paper
folder (optional)

1. **CUT THE PAPERS:** From the ivory pearl cardstock, cut a 4¼-inch square for the work piece. From the ivory cardstock, cut a rectangle 5¼ x 10½ inches for the base card. From the mottled green/brown/ivory paper cut a 4¾-inch square. From the textured metallic gold/silver paper, cut a 5-inch square.

2. Score and fold the ivory base card (page 16) in half to form a 5¼-inch square.

3. Following the instructions in Getting Started (page 13), transfer the embroidery pattern to the ivory pearl work piece, making the necessary perforations.

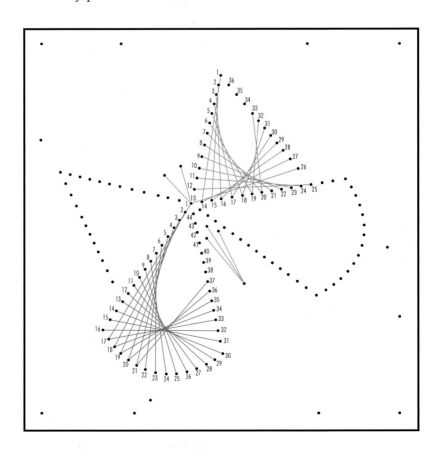

4. **EMBROIDER THE PATTERN:** With the pattern markings to guide you, stitch the top right wing using the gold metallic thread: Come out at hole 1 and go into hole 14. Continue stitching in the following sequence: hole 15 − 2, 3 − 16, 17 − 4, 5 − 18, 19 − 6, 7 − 20, 21 − 8, 9 − 22, 23 − 10, 11 − 24, 25 − 12, 13 − 26, 27 − 14, 15 − 28, 29 − 16, 17 − 30, 31 − 18, 19 − 32, 33 − 20, 21 − 34, 35 − 22, 23 − 36, 1 − 24. Repeat to stitch the top left wing.

5. Using the variegated thread, stitch the bottom right wing: Come out at hole 1 and go into hole 17. Continue stitching in the following sequence: 18 − 2, 3 − 19, 20 − 4, 5 − 21, 22 − 6, 7 − 23, 24 − 8, 9 − 25, 26 − 10, 11 − 27, 28 − 12, 13 − 29, 30 − 14, 15 − 31, 32 − 16, 17 − 33, 34 − 18, 19 − 35, 36 − 20, 21 − 37, 38 − 22, 23 − 39, 40 − 24, 25 − 41, 42 − 26, 27 − 43, 44 − 28, 29 − 45, 1 − 30. Repeat to stitch the bottom left wing. Outline the top wings with the variegated thread.

6. Using the gold metallic braid, stitch the antennae, body, and two points of the bottom wings. Stitch the corners of the work piece with the variegated thread as shown.

7. Center and mount the completed work piece (page 16) onto the mottled green/brown/ivory square using double-sided tape. Similarly mount these layers onto the textured metallic gold/silver square. To finish, center and mount all layers onto the front of the base card.

Bell

Simply follow the numerical sequence of stitches to create this beautiful bell design, which can be used to grace a card to send Christmas or wedding wishes to very special people.

YOU'LL NEED

PAPERS

Cardstock: black, gold pearl, ivory (8½ x 11 sheets)

EMBELLISHMENTS

Variegated gold/green/red metallic thread

Gold metallic thread #4 braid

SUPPLIES

Corner punch

Hand-sewing needle

Glue stick

Removable tape

Double-sided tape

Scissors

Pencil

Paper cutter or craft knife and metal ruler

Perforating tool

Craft foam (12 x 18-inch sheet)

Scoring tool and bone paper folder (optional)

1. **CUT THE CARDSTOCK:** From the black cardstock, cut a 4¾-inch square for the work piece. From the gold pearl, cut a 5-inch square. From the ivory, cut a rectangle 5¼ x 10½ inches for the base card.

2. Score and fold the ivory base card (page 16) in half to form a 5¼-inch square.

3. Following the instructions in Getting Started (page 13), transfer the embroidery pattern to the black work piece, making the necessary perforations.

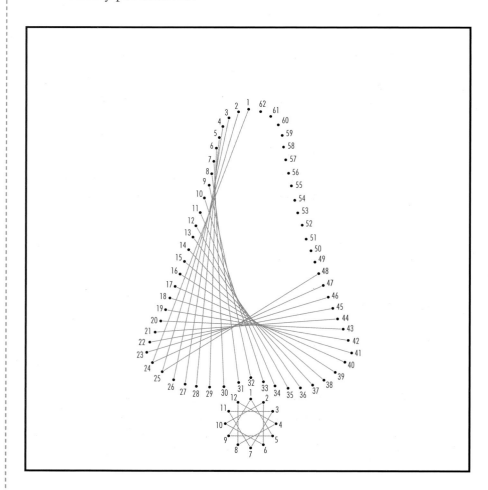

4. **EMBROIDER THE PATTERN:** With the pattern markings to guide you, and using the variegated gold/green/red metallic thread, stitch the bell counterclockwise, making sure not to miss any holes. To begin, come out at hole 1 and go into hole 24. From there, continue stitching in the following sequence: 25 − 2, 3 − 26, 27 − 4, 5 − 28, 29 − 6, 7 − 30, 31 − 8, 9 − 32, 33 − 10, 11 − 34, 35 − 12, 13 − 36, 37 − 14, 15 − 38, 39 − 16, 17 − 40, 41 − 18, 19 − 42, 43 − 20, 21 − 44, 45 − 22, 23 − 46, 47 − 24, 25 − 48, 49 − 26, 27 − 50, 51 − 28, 29 − 52, 53 − 30, 31 − 54, 55 − 32, 33 − 56, 57 − 34, 35 − 58, 59 − 36, 37 − 60, 61 − 38, 39 − 62, 1 − 40, 41 − 2, 3 − 42, 43 − 4, 5 − 44, 45 − 6, 7 − 46, 47 − 8, 9 − 48, 49 − 10, 11 − 50, 51 − 12, 13 − 52, 53 − 14, 15 − 54, 55 − 16, 17 − 56, 57 − 18, 19 − 58, 59 − 20, 21 − 60, 61 − 22, 23 − 62. Using a double strand of thread, outline the bottom of the bell in backstitches.

5. To stitch the hanging clapper, come out at hole 1 and go into hole 5. From there, stitch from 6 − 2, 3 − 7, 8 − 4, 5 − 9, 10 − 6, 7 − 11, 12 − 8, 9 − 1, 2 − 10, 11 − 3, 4 − 12.

6. **MAKE THE BOW:** Using a double strand of the gold metallic thread, wrap it around three fingers four times. Slip it off your fingers and tie it in a knot in the center to fashion a simple bow. Attach the bow to the top of the bell by stitching through the knot into two or three perforations. Secure the end of the thread to the back of the work piece with tape.

7. **COMPLETE THE WORK PIECE:** Use a corner punch to decoratively cut the four corners of the framed work piece; reserve the cut pieces.

8. Center and mount the completed work piece (page 16) onto the gold pearl square using double-sided tape. Glue the reserved corners from the work piece onto the corners of the gold pearl square. To finish, center and mount these layers onto the front of the base card using double-sided tape.

VARIATION

Create a simpler bell by stitching the bell counterclockwise as in step 4, but stop after stitching 1 − 40. For this version do not outline the bottom of the bell in backstitches. To form the clapper on the bottom, make stitches straight across the diameter of the circle until all the holes are filled. Attach a small ribbon bow at the top.

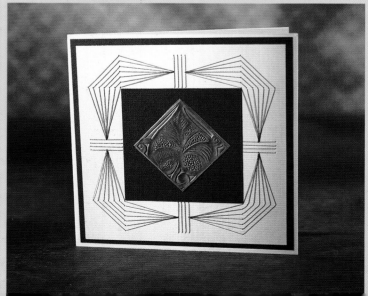

2

Medallions and Borders

BEFORE YOU BEGIN

If you're like most craftspeople, you're probably hanging on to hoards of paper and fabric scraps, random stickers, and other decorative elements left over from projects past. Some may have interesting textures or beautiful patterns that you'd like to use again but don't have enough of for them to be the primary material of other projects. These odds and ends are just the thing to make eye-catching center medallions for greeting cards. Depending on the material, they can be glued to the front of the card, such as Pewter Leaf (page 46) and Faux Tile (page 48), or taped behind a window cut in a piece of cardstock and mounted onto the card, as in Windowpane (page 50) and Flying Cranes (page 56).

Embroidered borders, beads, and punched corners are among the embellishments that can be added to enhance the decorative quality of these medallions. Designing a border specifically to suit the center motif, as was done with Asian Leaves (page 54), can be particularly effective. Most of the embroidered border patterns in this chapter can be used with any center design and technique found in this book.

For some of the projects in the chapter it will be necessary to cut out a square or circle from the center of the work piece. To make this task easy, we recommend using any of the shape cutters available at your local arts and crafts store. If you have a steady hand, you can use a template or ruler and a craft knife or other cutting tool to draw and cut out the shapes. Always cut out the shape before stitching the pattern to avoid the possibility of cutting into the stitches. Use the pattern perforations on the work piece as a guide to centering the cutouts or layering the papers.

Lime Flowers

Two flower medallions contained in embroidered squares are the focal points of this any-occasion springtime card. The design works with the rectangular shape, allowing the card to be used horizontally or vertically.

YOU'LL NEED

PAPERS

Cardstock: lime green, gold pearl, white (8½ x 11-inch sheets)

Lime green floral paper

EMBELLISHMENTS

Variegated gold/green metallic thread #4 braid

Gold metallic thread #4 braid

SUPPLIES

Hand-sewing needle

Removable tape

Double-sided tape

Glue stick

Scissors

Pencil

Paper cutter or craft knife and metal ruler

Craft foam (12 x 18-inch sheet)

Perforating tool

Scoring tool and bone paper folder (optional)

1. **CUT THE PAPERS:** From the lime green cardstock, cut a rectangle 3½ x 6 inches for the work piece. From the gold pearl cardstock, cut a rectangle 4 x 6½ inches. From the white cardstock, cut a rectangle 6¾ x 8½ inches for the base card and two 1½-inch squares. From

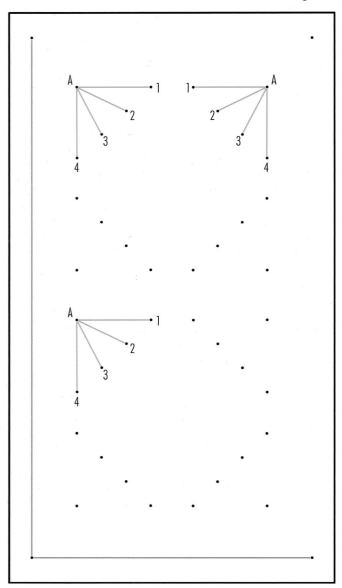

the lime green floral paper, cut two 1¼-inch squares, making sure to have a motif in each square.

2. Score and fold the white base card (page 16) in half to form a rectangle 4¼ x 6¾ inches.

3. Following the instructions in Getting Started (page 13), transfer the embroidery pattern to the lime green work piece, making the necessary perforations.

4. **EMBROIDER THE PATTERNS:** With the pattern markings to guide you, stitch the four corners of the interior squares: Using the variegated gold/green thread, come out hole A and stitch into holes 1–4, always returning to A to start each new stitch. Continue around the square until all corners are stitched. Carry the thread to the next square and stitch each of the corners in the same manner.

5. Using the gold metallic thread, stitch from corner to corner to make the rectangular border.

6. **MOUNT THE MEDALLIONS:** Glue the two floral squares onto the two white squares. Center and mount these squares (page 16) on point in the center of the stitched squares of the work piece using double-sided tape.

7. Center and mount the work piece onto the gold pearl rectangle using double-sided tape. To finish, center and mount these layers onto the front of the base card.

Pewter Leaf

A beautiful embossed pewter sticker draws the eye to the center of this card. To enhance the drama, a delicate silvery frame is embroidered in a geometric pattern that captures the sharp angles of the medallion.

YOU'LL NEED

PAPERS

Cardstock: white, navy blue
(8½ x 11-inch sheets: 2 white, 1 navy blue)

EMBELLISHMENTS

Blue/black twist metallic thread

Pewter or silver sticker with raised leaf design or design of your choice (1½ inches square)

SUPPLIES

Hand-sewing needle

Removable tape

Double-sided tape

Scissors

Pencil

Paper cutter or craft knife and metal ruler

Craft foam (12 x 18-inch sheet)

Perforating tool

Scoring tool and bone paper folder (optional)

1. **CUT THE CARDSTOCK:** From the white, cut a 4¾-inch square for the work piece and a rectangle 5¼ x 10½ inches for the base card. From the navy blue, cut a 2¾-inch square and a 5-inch square.

2. Score and fold the white base card (page 16) in half to form a 5¼-inch square.

3. Following the instructions in Getting Started (page 13), transfer the embroidery pattern to the white work piece, making the necessary perforations.

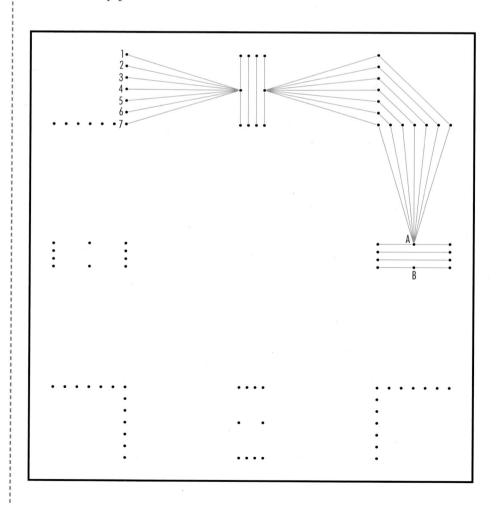

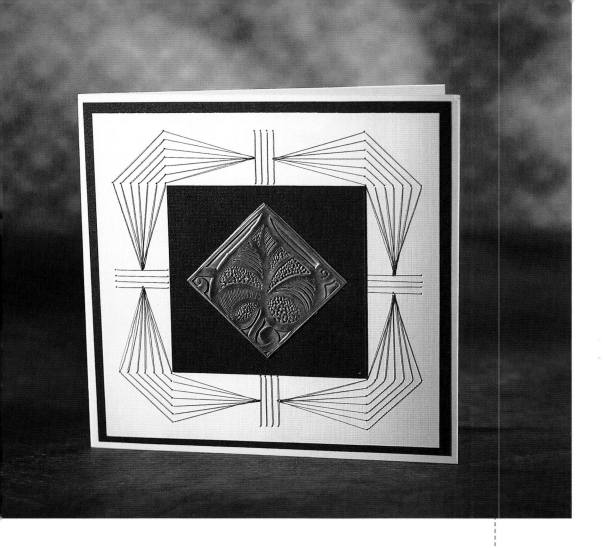

4. **EMBROIDER THE PATTERN:** With the pattern markings to guide you, stitch each side of the work piece. Complete one side before moving on to the next. Using the blue/black twist metallic thread, come out at hole A and go into holes 1–7 closest to it, always returning to A to start each new stitch. Repeat from hole B to stitch the second half of each side. Then stitch the four parallel lines between the two halves.

5. At each corner stitch diagonal lines as shown to join the sides.

6. **COMPLETE THE WORK PIECE:** Peel the backing from the sticker and affix it, on point, to the center of the small navy square. Center and mount the small navy square onto the stitched work piece using double-sided tape.

7. Center and mount the completed work piece (page 16) onto the large navy square using double-sided tape. To finish, similarly center and mount all layers onto the front of the base card.

Faux Tile

Three-dimensional objects, such as this acrylic tile, will turn a card into a handsome handmade gift. The crosshatched border is easy to stitch and can add interest to any simple card.

YOU'LL NEED

PAPERS

Cardstock: black, gold, beige
(8½ x 11-inch sheets)

Metallic lime green decorative paper

EMBELLISHMENTS

Gold metallic thread

Decorative green self-sticking faux tile or sticker
(2 inches square)

SUPPLIES

Hand-sewing needle

Removable tape

Double-sided tape

White craft glue

Scissors

Pencil

Paper cutter or craft knife with metal ruler

Craft foam (12 x 18-inch sheet)

Perforating tool

Scoring tool and bone paper folder (optional)

1. **CUT THE PAPERS:** From the black cardstock, cut a 4¾-inch square for the work piece. From the gold cardstock cut a 2¾-inch square. From the beige cardstock, cut a rectangle 5¼ x 10½ inches for the base card. From the metallic lime green paper, cut a 5-inch square.

2. Score and fold the beige base card (page 16) in half to form a 5¼-inch square.

3. Following the instructions in Getting Started (page 13), transfer the embroidery pattern to the black work piece, making the necessary perforations.

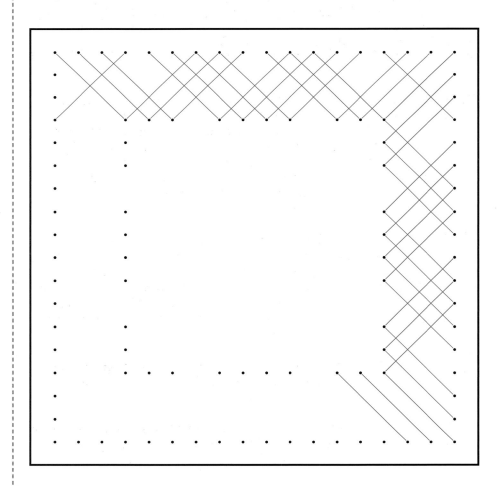

——— layer 1
——— layer 2

4. **EMBROIDER THE PATTERN:** With the pattern markings to guide you, stitch the crosshatched border using the gold metallic thread. Working clockwise, stitch the bottom layer of crosshatches first (layer 1). Beginning at the top left of one side, stitch diagonally to the right in the following sequence: stitch 3, skip 1, stitch 4, skip 1, stitch 3. Turn the card clockwise and stitch the next side in the same manner. Repeat the stitching-and-turning sequence on the remaining two sides to complete the bottom layer.

5. Working counterclockwise, stitch the top layer of crosshatches (layer 2). Beginning at the top right of one side, stitch diagonally to the left in the following sequence: skip 1, stitch 2, skip 1, stitch 4, skip 1, stitch 3, skip 2, stitch 1. Turn the card counterclockwise and stitch the next side in the same manner. Repeat the stitching-and-turning sequence on the remaining two sides to complete the top layer of the crosshatch border.

6. **MOUNT THE TILE:** Center and mount the gold square (page 16) onto the center of the work piece, inside the stitched border. Glue the tile to the center of the gold square.

7. Center and mount the work piece with the tile onto the lime green paper using double-sided tape. To finish, mount these layers onto the front of the beige base card in the same manner.

Windowpane

Like looking out your window into the garden on a fine summer day, a similar view greets the recipient of this cheery card. The delicate stitched flowers bring a bit of the garden inside the window.

YOU'LL NEED

PAPERS

Cardstock: white, forest green, sage green (8½ x 11-inch sheets)

EMBELLISHMENTS

Scrap of fabric with a floral design or outdoor scene (3¾ inches square)

Variegated gold/green/pink metallic thread

Red metallic thread

Green metallic thread

SUPPLIES

Hand-sewing needle

Tapes: removable, transparent, double-sided

Scissors

Pencil

Paper cutter or craft knife and metal ruler

Craft foam (12 x 18-inch sheet)

Perforating tool

Scoring tool and bone paper folder (optional)

1. **CUT THE CARDSTOCK:** From the white, cut a 4¾-inch square for the work piece. From the forest green, cut a 5-inch square. From the sage green, cut a rectangle 5¼ x 10½ inches for the base card.

2. Score and fold the sage green base card (page 16) in half to form a 5¼-inch square.

3. Following the instructions in Getting Started (page 13), transfer the embroidery pattern to the white work piece, making the necessary perforations.

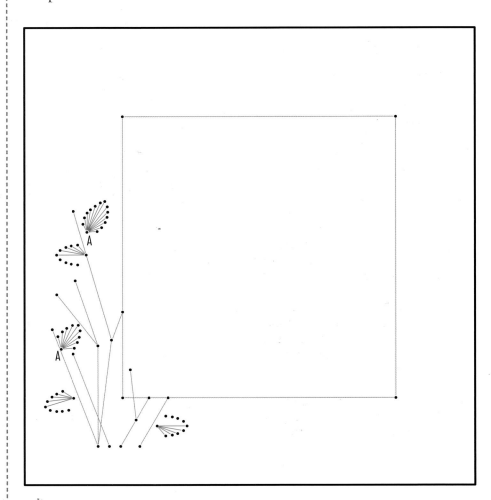

4. **PREPARE THE WORK PIECE:**
Turn the work piece wrong side up, and using the perforations that form the center square as guidelines and a ruler, draw a 2¾-inch square centered inside. Draw a 1¼-inch square in each corner of the 2¾-inch square; these are the windowpanes. Cut out the windowpanes using a craft knife or cutting tool. Turn the work piece right side up.

5. **EMBROIDER THE PATTERN:**
With the pattern markings to guide you, stitch the stems and branches of the flowers using the variegated metallic thread. Using the same thread, stitch the outline of the window from corner to corner.

6. Using the red metallic thread, stitch the two red leaves: Come out at hole A and stitch the ribs of the leaves clockwise, returning to A at the start of each new stitch. Using the green metallic thread, stitch the remaining three leaves in the same manner.

7. **COMPLETE THE WORK PIECE:** Place the work piece on the right side of the fabric and move it around until the desired image shows through the windowpanes. Secure the fabric in position on the back of the work piece using transparent tape. The fabric should be taut.

8. Center and mount the completed work piece (page 16) onto the forest green square using double-sided tape. To finish, center and mount all layers onto the front of the base card.

Small Trifold

This trifold card with its cutout windows and beaded embroidery is the perfect size for a gift enclosure or brief note.

YOU'LL NEED

PAPERS

Cardstock: lime green, medium blue, white (8½ x 11-inch sheets)

Decorative lime green paper

EMBELLISHMENTS

Variegated blue/green metallic thread #4 braid

Lime green metallic thread #4 braid

Blue seed beads (28)

Green seed beads (20)

SUPPLIES

Templates for 1¼- and 2-inch squares and cutting tool

Hand-sewing and beading needles

Removable tape

Double-sided tape

Scissors

Pencil

Paper cutter or craft knife and metal ruler

Craft foam (12 x 18-inch sheet)

Perforating tool

Scoring tool and bone paper folder (optional)

1. **CUT THE PAPERS:** From the lime green cardstock, cut a rectangle 3½ x 4 inches for the first work piece. From the medium blue cardstock, cut a rectangle 3½ x 4 inches for the second work piece. From the white cardstock, cut a rectangle 10½ x 4 inches for the base card. From the decorative lime green paper, cut a 1½-inch square.

2. Following the instructions in Getting Started (page 13), transfer the embroidery patterns to the lime green and blue work pieces, making the necessary perforations.

3. **PREPARE THE BASE CARD:** Score the white base card (page 16) every 3½ inches and fold each section to the center to create a trifold. Using the templates or a ruler and cutting tool, carefully measure and cut out a 2-inch square from the center of the first section of the trifolded base card. Cut a 1¼-inch square from the center of the third section.

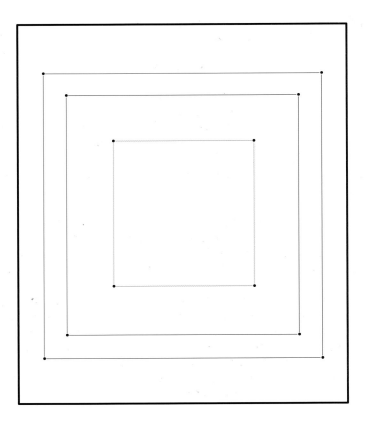

4. **PREPARE THE WORK PIECES:** Using the perforations as a guide and the templates and cutting tool, carefully measure and cut out a 2-inch square from the center of the lime green work piece and a 1¼-inch square from the center of the blue work piece.

5. **EMBROIDER THE PATTERN:** With the pattern markings to guide you, stitch the borders of the lime green work piece using the variegated metallic thread. Stitch the inner border from corner to corner. Use the beading needle to stitch the outer border: Slip seven blue beads onto the thread and stitch one side. Repeat, slipping on another seven beads as you begin to stitch each of the remaining three sides.

6. Using the lime green metallic thread and the beading needle, stitch the border of the blue work piece: Slip five green beads onto the thread and stitch one side. Repeat, slipping on another five green beads as you begin to stitch each of the remaining three sides.

7. Center, align, and mount the lime green work piece (page 16) onto the front of the first section of the trifolded base card using double-sided tape. Glue the lime green decorative paper behind the window cut into the blue work piece and center, align, and mount this onto the front of the third section of the trifold. To finish, fold the card so that the blue cardstock shows through the window cut into the lime green cardstock.

Asian Leaves

The Oriental style of this border was chosen to offset the lovely Asian design on the fabric seen in the window cut into the center of the cardstock. Notice how the embroidery pattern echoes the leaves on the tree.

YOU'LL NEED

PAPERS

Cardstock: black, red, gold pearl, ivory (8½ x 11 sheets)

EMBELLISHMENTS

Scrap of fabric with Asian motif (3 inches square)

Red metallic thread

Gold metallic thread

SUPPLIES

Template for 2-inch square and cutting tool

Hand-sewing needle

Tapes: removable, transparent, double-sided tape

Scissors

Pencil

Paper cutter or craft knife with metal ruler

Craft foam (12 x 18-inch sheet)

Perforating tool

Scoring tool and bone paper folder (optional)

1. **CUT THE CARDSTOCK:** From the black, cut a 4½-inch square for the work piece. From the red cut a 4¾-inch square. From the gold pearl, cut a 5-inch square. From the ivory, cut a rectangle 5¼ x 10½ inches for the base card.

2. Score and fold the ivory base card (page 16) in half to form a 5¼-inch square.

3. Following the instructions in Getting Started (page 13), transfer the embroidery pattern to the black work piece, making the necessary perforations.

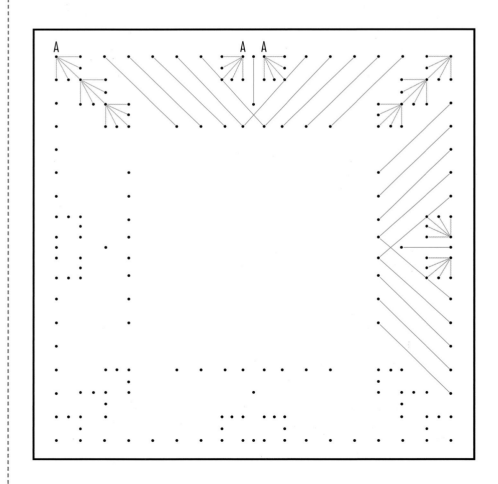

4. **PREPARE THE WORK PIECE:** Using the perforations as a guide and the template and cutting tool, carefully draw and cut out a 2-inch square from the center on the wrong side of the work piece. Turn the work piece right side up.

5. **EMBROIDER THE PATTERN:** With the pattern markings to guide you, stitch the parallel diagonal lines on each side of the work piece. Complete one side of the border before moving on to the next. Using the red metallic thread, and working from left to right, stitch five parallel diagonal lines toward the center, then repeat to stitch five diagonal lines from right to left. The fourth lines will meet at the inside of the border and the fifth lines will cross. Stitch the short vertical line in the center of the diagonals. Continue stitching the remaining sides of the border in the same manner.

6. Beginning in one corner, stitch the leaves: Using the gold metallic thread, come out at hole A of the first leaf and go into holes 1–5, always returning to A to start each new stitch. The second and third leaves use the middle stitch of the previous leaf as their starting point. From there, stitch the remaining two corner leaves as you did the first. From behind the work piece, carry the thread to the center and stitch the two leaves from hole A to holes 1–5, as you did the first corner leaf. Continue around the border until all leaves are stitched.

7. **COMPLETE THE WORK PIECE:** Place the opening of the work piece on the right side of the fabric and move it around until it frames the part of the motif you want to show through the window. Secure the fabric in position on the back of the work piece using transparent tape. The fabric should be taut.

8. Center and mount the work piece (page 16) onto the red cardstock square using double-sided tape. Similarly center and mount these pieces onto the gold pearl square. To finish, center and mount all layers onto the front of the base card.

TIP

A beautiful fabric or paper with an interesting design or textural pattern can be the inspiration for a card. Select the cardstock colors and textures to complement your chosen fabric or paper. A window cut into the card helps to hide any frayed edges. The embroidered border can reflect the theme of the design or any part of the pattern.

Flying Cranes

The rich inks of the chiyogami paper used for the center medallion give this card a regal elegance, an effect that is aided by the Chinese-inspired colors of the cardstock and the decoratively cut corners.

YOU'LL NEED

PAPERS

Cardstock: black, red, gold pearl, (8½ x 11 sheets: 2 black, 1 gold, 1 red)

Chiyogami or other decorative paper with Chinese crane pattern or pattern of your choice

EMBELLISHMENT

Gold metallic thread

SUPPLIES

Template for a 2-inch circle and cutting tool

Decorative corner punch

Hand-sewing needle

Tapes: removable, transparent, double-sided

Glue stick

Scissors

Pencil

Paper cutter or craft knife and metal ruler

Craft foam (12 x 18-inch sheet)

Perforating tool

Scoring tool and bone paper folder (optional)

1. **CUT THE PAPERS:** From the black cardstock, cut a 4¾-inch square for the work piece and a rectangle 5¼ x 10½ inches for the base card. From the red cardstock cut a 4¾-inch square. From the gold pearl cardstock, cut a 5-inch square. From the crane-patterned paper, cut a 3-inch square.

2. Score and fold the black base card (page 16) in half to form a 5¼-inch square.

3. Following the instructions in Getting Started (page 13), transfer the embroidery pattern to the black work piece, making the necessary perforations.

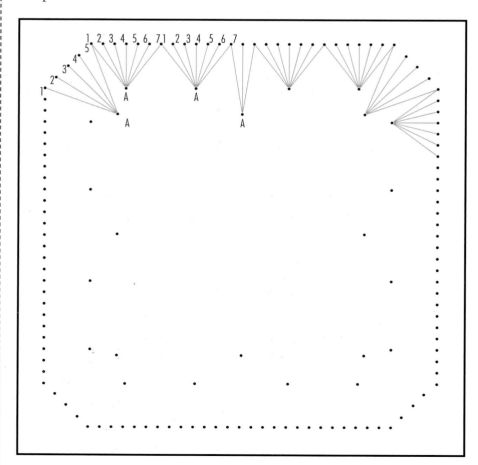

4. **PREPARE THE WORK PIECE:** Using the perforations as a guide and the template and cutting tool, carefully draw and cut out a 2-inch circle from the center on the wrong side of the work piece. Turn the work piece right side up.

5. **EMBROIDER THE PATTERN:** With the marked pattern as your guide, stitch the border, beginning with the triangle at the top left corner. Using the gold metallic thread, come out at hole A and stitch to the five holes on the outer edge of the pattern, always returning to hole A to start each new stitch. Working clockwise around the border, continue stitching in this manner, from each hole A to the holes on the outer edge of each triangle. Notice that the last stitch of each triangle shares a hole with the first stitch of the next.

6. **COMPLETE THE WORK PIECE:** Place the cutout opening of the work piece on the right side of the crane-patterned paper and move it around until it frames the part of the motif you want to show through the window. Secure the patterned paper in position on the back of the work piece using transparent tape.

7. Using the corner punch, decoratively cut the four corners of the work piece.

8. Center and mount the work piece (page 16) onto the red square using double-sided tape, so that the red is showing only in the corners and the sides are perfectly aligned. Center and mount these layers onto the gold pearl square using double-sided tape. To finish, center and mount all layers onto the front of the base card.

3

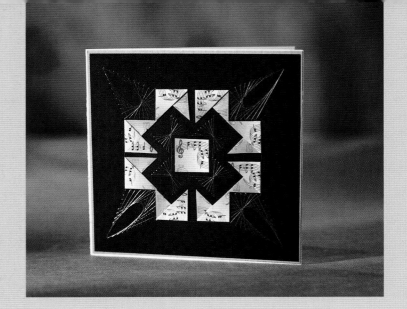

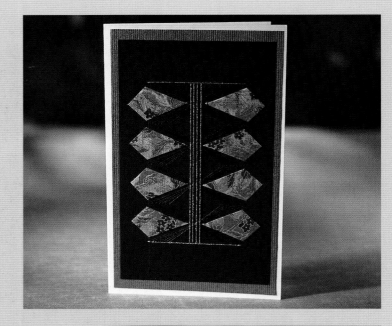

Teabag Folding

BEFORE YOU BEGIN

Originated in The Netherlands, teabag folding is a technique similar to origami. Traditionally the pretty printed paper sleeves that held teabags were cut into squares, identically folded, and glued together to form a medallion or pasted on paper to create a decorative design.

Nowadays there's no need to drink countless cups of tea in order to make a card. You can purchase sheets of teabag folding papers in crafts-supply stores or download the printed patterns from various teabag folding sites on the Internet. The printed sheets contain identical 1½-inch squares in an endless array of patterns and designs. The printed teabag papers imported from Europe are lighter than standard bond paper and make folding easier. They also don't show the creases when folded, so if you make a mistake you can unfold and try again without the confusion of seeing previous crease lines. Teabag folding also works well on origami and chiyogami papers as well as on other lightweight papers that have repeating designs. Select the teabag papers for your cards first, then choose cardstock to complement the colors of the papers.

In this chapter, basic teabag folds are made on different papers and combined with embroidery to make these distinctive cards. As in previous chapters, the stitching is done first and is a helpful guide for placing the teabag papers. Experiment using papers of different weights as you try teabag folding.

When working with teabag papers, it is important that the squares be cut precisely and they all be exactly the same size. When folding the papers, be sure the design is always facing the same direction when you start and that all the squares are folded the same way. The papers are meant to look identical once folded. This is especially necessary when the papers are to be glued together to make a design, such the Design in Black and White (page 66). Some people like to go over the folds with a bone paper folder or a butter knife to get sharp creases. The more precise you are when cutting out the squares and folding them the neater the project will turn out.

Dragon Face

The three different folds used to create the dragon faces on this card are good examples of why it is important to cut and fold the teabag papers precisely.

YOU'LL NEED

PAPERS

Cardstock: olive green, black, metallic green, and ivory (8½ x 11-inch sheets: 2 black, 1 each of the others)

Decorative paper printed with Chinese characters

Teabag folding papers with dragon or other Oriental design (six 1½-inch squares with borders intact)

EMBELLISHMENT

Antique gold metallic thread #4 braid

SUPPLIES

Hand-sewing needle

Removable tape

Double-sided tape

Glue stick

Scissors

Pencil

Paper cutter or craft knife and metal ruler

Craft foam (12 x 18-inch sheet)

Perforating tool

Scoring tool and bone paper folder (optional)

1. **CUT THE PAPERS:** From the olive green cardstock, cut a rectangle 3½ x 6¼ inches for the work piece. From the black cardstock, cut a rectangle 2 x 6 inches and one 4½ x 6¾ inches and a strip 1 x 4⅞ inches. From the metallic green cardstock, cut a rectangle 4¼ x 6½ inches. From the ivory cardstock, cut a rectangle 7 x 9½ inches for the base card. From the decorative paper, cut a strip ¾ x 4¾ inches.

2. Score and fold the ivory base card (page 16) in half to form a rectangle 7 x 4¾ inches.

3. Following the instructions in Getting Started (page 13), transfer the embroidery pattern to the olive green work piece, making the necessary perforations.

4. **EMBROIDER THE PATTERN:** With the pattern markings to guide you, and using the antique gold metallic thread, come out at hole A, the topmost perforation, and make a long stitch into hole B. Next, make small stitches from holes 1–3, going into hole B to complete each stitch. Then make a long stitch from B into the second hole A to complete the first triangle. Continue stitching in the same manner—one long, three short, one long—down the length of the work piece to make nine connected triangles with points alternating right and left.

5. **CONSTRUCT THE DECORATIVE LAYER OF THE CARD:** Use the photograph to guide you through steps 5 to 7. Mount the 2 x 6-inch black rectangle (page 16) onto the left side of the embroidered work piece using double-sided tape.

6. Center and mount the decorative paper strip onto the slightly larger black strip using double-sided tape. Center and mount this piece on the right side of the metallic green rectangle.

7. Center and mount the work piece on the left side of the metallic green rectangle, slightly covering the decorative strip on the right. Cut a ¾-inch square from the two right corners of the metallic green rectangle, framing the decorative paper on that side.

8. Review Before You Begin at the start of this chapter.

9. **MAKE THE TEABAG FOLDS:** Begin by making sure the pattern on each of the teabag papers is facing the same direction, then turn the papers over so the white (unprinted) side is facing up. For the top dragon face on the card, fold two teabag paper squares in half diagonally from bottom left corner to top right corner (see figure 1), so that one half of the dragon face is shown on each folded paper. Set this face aside.

10. For the middle dragon face, cut one teabag in half horizontally so that the top of the dragon's face is on one half and the bottom of the dragon's face is on the other. Cut another square in half vertically so that the left side of the face is on one half and the right side of the face is on the other. Place the four cut halves on the work surface with the border on the bottom. Turn the halves over so that the white side is facing up, making sure the black border is still on the bottom. Fold them in half vertically; unfold. Fold the sides of each half down to the center crease to make a triangle (figure 2). This will result in four triangles, each showing one quarter of the dragon's face.

11. For the bottom dragon, fold the remaining two squares in half diagonally from bottom right to top left (figure 3). Trim off any excess white paper showing on the completed folded shapes.

12. **PLACE THE TEABAG DESIGN:** Using the photograph as a guide, arrange the folded triangles of each of the dragon faces on the black strip taped to the work piece. Make sure the individual pieces of each face fit neatly together with about $\frac{1}{16}$ inch of space between. Evenly space and center the three faces. Glue the folded triangles in place to complete the faces.

13. Center and mount the completed decorated layer onto the $4\frac{1}{2} \times 6\frac{3}{4}$-inch black rectangle using double-sided tape. To finish, similarly center and mount these layers onto the front of the base card.

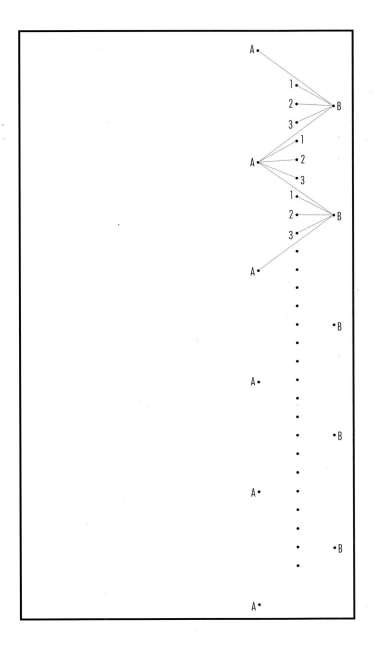

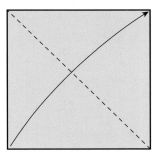

FIGURE 1

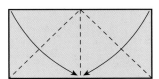

FIGURE 2

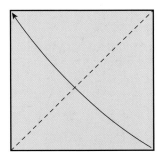

FIGURE 3

Oriental Red and Gold

The bright red and gold print of the chiyogami paper used in this project makes the design stand out on this very simple card. In keeping with the Chinese motif, the embroidered square with beads is meant to resemble an abacus.

YOU'LL NEED

PAPERS

Cardstock: gold pearl, black, white (8½ x 11-inch sheets)

Red chiyogami paper with Chinese characters

EMBELLISHMENTS

Gold metallic thread #4 braid

Black/copper blending filament

Copper seed beads (12)

SUPPLIES

Hand-sewing and beading needles

Removable tape

Double-sided tape

Glue stick

Scissors

Pencil

Paper cutter or craft knife and metal ruler

Craft foam (12 x 18-inch sheet)

Perforating tool

Scoring tool and bone paper folder (optional)

TIP
This particular fold can be used as picture corners on greeting cards or scrapbook pages.

1. **CUT THE PAPERS:** From the gold pearl cardstock, cut a 3½-inch square for the work piece. From the black cardstock, cut a 3¾-inch square. From the white cardstock, cut a rectangle 4 x 8 inches for the base card. From the chiyogami paper, cut a 1½-inch square and four ½ x 2½-inch strips.

2. Score and fold the white base card (page 16) in half to form a 4-inch square.

3. Following the instructions in Getting Started (page 13), transfer the embroidery pattern to the gold work piece, making the necessary perforations.

4. **EMBROIDER THE PATTERN:** With the pattern markings to guide you, stitch the three graduated squares in the center using the gold metallic thread. Stitch the same side of the graduated squares before moving on to the next side. Begin at the smallest square and stitch from left to right, then move to the next square and

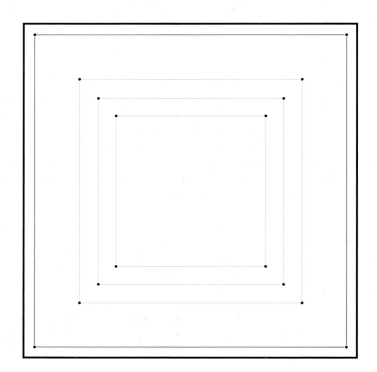

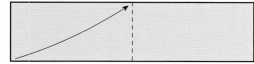

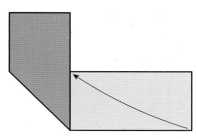

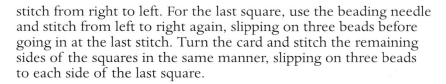

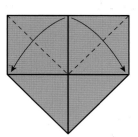

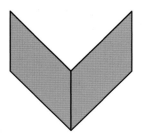

stitch from right to left. For the last square, use the beading needle and stitch from left to right again, slipping on three beads before going in at the last stitch. Turn the card and stitch the remaining sides of the squares in the same manner, slipping on three beads to each side of the last square.

5. Using a double strand of the black/copper blending filament, stitch the border square on the card. The stitched squares will serve as guides for placing the teabag folds.

6. Review Before You Begin at the start of this chapter.

7. **MAKE THE TEABAG FOLDS:** With the white (unprinted) side of the chiyogami paper facing up, fold one paper strip in half widthwise; unfold (figure 1). Next, fold the left side up to the center crease, then do the same on the right side (figure 2). Turn shape over. Fold the top of each side behind itself diagonally so the edges align (figure 3) to form a V shape (figure 4). Fold the remaining strips in the same manner. Trim off any excess white paper showing on the completed folded shapes.

8. **PLACE THE TEABAG DESIGN:** Glue the 1½-inch chiyogami square onto the center of the card, inside the smallest stitched square. Glue one finished teabag fold into each of the corners of the card between the outermost gold stitched square and the large black/copper stitched square.

9. Center and mount the finished work piece (page 16) onto the black cardstock square using double-sided tape. To finish, similarly center and mount these layers onto the front of the base card.

Design in Black and White

A very striking kaleidoscope effect is formed by gluing together the identical repeating pattern of each of the folded papers to make the eight-pointed medallion in the center of this graphically interesting card.

YOU'LL NEED

PAPERS

Cardstock: black, white (8½ x 11-inch sheets)

Decorative paper with a repeating pattern or teabag folding paper (one sheet)

EMBELLISHMENT

Bronze metallic thread #4 braid

SUPPLIES

Hand-sewing needle

Removable tape

Double-sided tape

Glue stick

Scissors

Pencil

Paper cutter or craft knife and metal ruler

Craft foam (12 x 18-inch sheet)

Perforating tool

Scoring tool and bone paper folder (optional)

1. **CUT THE PAPERS:** From the black cardstock, cut a 4½-inch square and a 3-inch square. From the white cardstock, cut a 3-inch square and a rectangle 4¾ x 9½ inches for the base card. From the decorative or teabag paper, cut a 4¼-inch square and eight 1½-inch squares, making sure the same design is in each of the eight squares.

2. Score and fold the white base card (page 16) in half to form a 4¾-inch square.

3. **CONSTRUCT THE WORK PIECE:** Center and mount (page 16) the 4¼-inch decorative paper square onto the 4½-inch black cardstock square using double-sided tape. Similarly center and mount the 3-inch black square onto the decorative paper on point so it resembles a diamond. Mount the 3-inch white cardstock square onto the black diamond, making sure it is centered and its sides are parallel to the sides of the decorative paper square.

4. **CREATE AND EMBROIDER THE STITCHING PATTERN:** Using the perforating tool, make a hole at each corner of both the black and white centered squares. Using the bronze metallic thread, stitch from corner to corner around the white square to outline it. In the same manner, stitch around the black square. The thread will cross over the white square at the corners.

5. Review Before You Begin at the start of this chapter.

6. **MAKE THE TEABAG FOLDS:** With the white (unprinted) side of the paper facing up, fold one 1½-inch decorative paper or teabag square in half, then in half again; unfold (figure 1). Next, fold the square in half diagonally in both directions; unfold (figure 2). Turn the paper over so the printed side is facing up. Place it on point and push the two sides in to the center along the diagonal crease to make a small folded square (figure 3). Place the small folded square on point and fold the top layer of the left side behind itself so that the point touches the center crease (figure 4). Repeat with the top layer of the right side (figure 5). Fold the remaining 1½-inch squares in the same manner. Trim off any excess white paper that shows on the completed folded shapes.

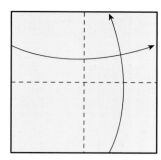

FIGURE 1

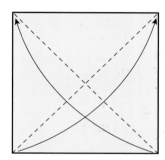

FIGURE 2

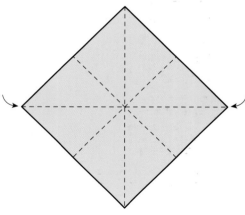

FIGURE 3

7. **PLACE THE TEABAG DESIGN:** Slide two folded shapes together so that the top fold of the first overlaps the top fold of the next and their bottom points meet (figure 6). Glue to secure in place. Continue placing and gluing the folded shapes together in this manner, one at a time, until all eight have been used to form a circle design. Glue the completed teabag design onto the white cardstock in the center of the card.

8. To finish, center and mount the completed work piece (page 16) onto the front of the base card using double-sided tape.

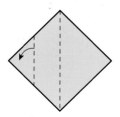

FIGURE 4

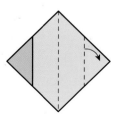

FIGURE 5

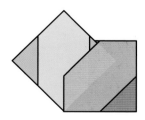

FIGURE 6

Kites and Pinwheels

Fanciful folded kites seem to have been carried by the wind to nestle between the blades of four sets of embroidered pinwheels on this card. Twilight shades of blue and mauve aid in fostering the illusion.

YOU'LL NEED

PAPERS

Cardstock: black, white (8½ x 11-inch sheets)

Metallic mauve decorative paper

Chiyogami paper with blue, mauve, and gold design

EMBELLISHMENTS

Variegated blue/black metallic thread

Mauve metallic thread #4 braid

SUPPLIES

Hand-sewing needle

Removable tape

Double-sided tape

Glue stick

Scissors

Pencil

Paper cutter or craft knife and metal ruler

Craft foam (12 x 18-inch sheet)

Perforating tool

Scoring tool and bone paper folder (optional)

1. **CUT THE PAPERS:** From the black cardstock, cut a rectangle 3½ x 6 inches for the work piece. From the white cardstock, cut a rectangle 6¾ x 8½ inches for the base card. From the mauve metallic paper, cut a rectangle 4 x 6½ inches. From the chiyogami paper, cut eight 1-inch squares.

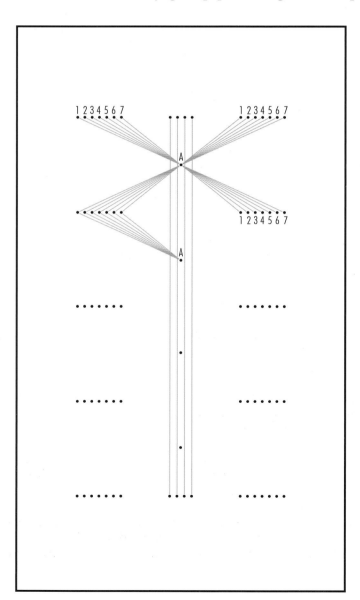

2. Score and fold the white base card (page 16) in half to form a rectangle 4¼ x 6¾ inches.

3. Following the instructions in Getting Started (page 13), transfer the embroidery pattern to the black work piece, making the necessary perforations.

4. **EMBROIDER THE PATTERN:** With the pattern markings to guide you, stitch the blades of the pinwheel. Using the variegated blue/black metallic thread, and beginning at the top of the pattern, come out at hole A and go into holes 1–7 on the left side of the card, always returning to A to start each new stitch. Using the same hole A, stitch into holes 1–7 on the right side of the card. Repeat to stitch the two pinwheel blades directly below the first two. Continue stitching down the card in this manner, until the four pinwheels are completed.

5. Using the mauve metallic thread, stitch the four vertical lines in the center of the card. Remember to always move to the next closest hole when stitching back and forth. Next, make a long horizontal stitch from blade to blade at the top of the card and at the bottom.

6. Review Before You Begin at the start of this chapter.

7. **MAKE THE TEABAG FOLDS:** With the white (unprinted) side of the paper facing up, fold one chiyogami square in half diagonally; unfold (figure 1). Holding the square so the crease is vertical, fold the left side to the crease. Repeat on the right side, making a kite shape (figure 2). Fold each of the remaining squares in the same manner. Trim off any excess white paper that shows on the completed folded shapes.

8. **PLACE THE TEABAG DESIGN:** Using the photograph as a guide, glue each kite shape between the blades of the pinwheels so there are four kite shapes per side.

9. Center and mount the completed work piece (page 16) onto the mauve metallic paper using double-sided tape. To finish, similarly center and mount these layers onto the front of the base card.

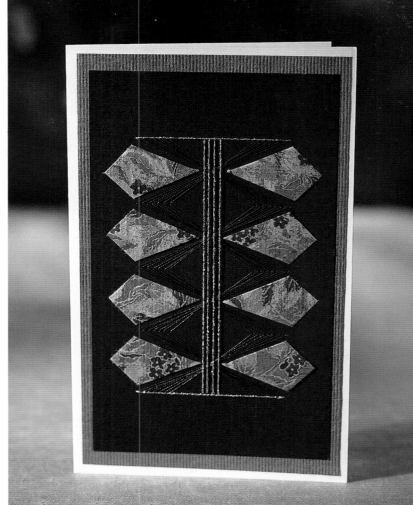

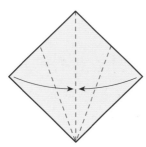

FIGURE 1

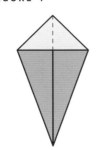

FIGURE 2

Wreath

This versatile design incorporates tiny teabag-folded and embroidered leaves into a wreath shape. Change the colors to fit the season to make cards for holidays all year round.

YOU'LL NEED

PAPERS

Cardstock: dark blue, sage green, ivory, or colors to match the teabag paper (8½ x 11-inch sheets)

Paisley teabag papers or any symmetrical design (four 1½-inch squares)

EMBELLISHMENT

Variegated pink/blue/silver metallic thread

SUPPLIES

Hand-sewing needle

Removable tape

Double-sided tape

Glue stick

Scissors

Pencil

Paper cutter or craft knife and metal ruler

Craft foam (12 x 18-inch sheet)

Perforating tool

Scoring tool and bone paper folder (optional)

1. **CUT THE PAPERS:** From the dark blue cardstock, cut a 4¾-inch square for the work piece. From the sage green cardstock, cut a 5-inch square. From the ivory cardstock, cut a rectangle 5¼ x 10½ inches for the base card.

2. Score and fold the ivory base card (page 16) in half to form a 5¼-inch square.

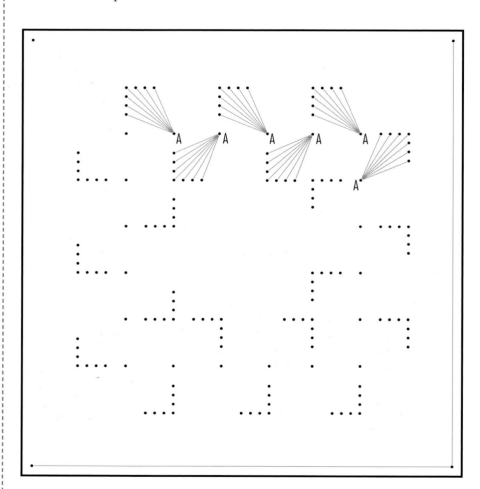

3. Following the instructions in Getting Started (page 13), transfer the embroidery pattern to the dark blue work piece, making the necessary perforations.

4. **EMBROIDER THE PATTERN:** With the pattern markings to guide you, stitch the leaves on the wreath. Using the variegated pink/blue/silver metallic thread, come out at hole A and go into holes 1–7 in numerical order, always returning to A to start the next stitch. Continue around the wreath, sewing each leaf in the same manner. When the leaves are completed, outline the border, stitching from corner to corner, using the same thread.

5. Review Before You Begin at the start of this chapter.

6. **CUT THE TEABAG PAPERS:** Fold each teabag paper square in half, white (unprinted) side facing up, then in half again (figure 1). Unfold, then cut each square along the creases into four ¾-inch squares to end up with 16 small squares. Arrange the small squares in four neat piles, each containing squares from the same quadrant of the original teabag paper. It will help to have them organized when they are glued onto the card to make a repeating pattern.

7. **MAKE THE TEABAG FOLDS:** Making sure the design of each square from the same quadrant is facing in the same direction, fold each of the ¾-inch squares as follows: With the white (unprinted) side facing up, fold the square on the diagonal from left to right to form a triangle (figure 2). With the fold of the triangle at the bottom, fold the left point up along the center line (figure 3). Fold the right point up along the center line (figure 4). Then take each point and fold it down so they meet the adjacent corners of the folded square (figures 5 and 6). Fold all sixteen squares in the same manner. Trim off any excess white paper showing on the completed folded shapes.

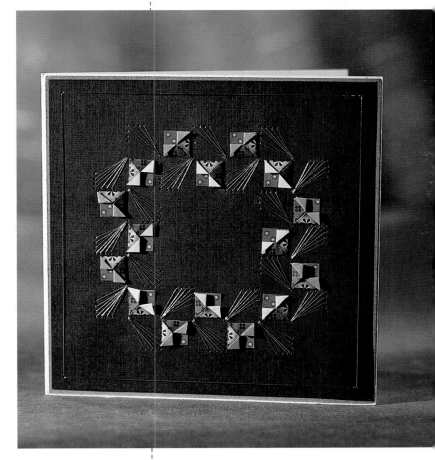

8. **PLACE THE TEABAG DESIGN:** Using the photograph to guide you, glue one teabag square in the spaces between the stitched leaves. Decide which direction the teabag folds should face, toward the center of the wreath or toward the outside. Most likely there will be four different patterns (or colors) showing on the folded pieces, so arrange them in a pleasing repeat-pattern design.

9. Center and mount the completed work piece (page 16) onto the green cardstock square using double-sided tape. To finish, similarly center and mount all layers onto the ivory base card.

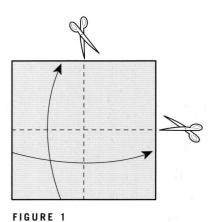

FIGURE 1

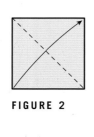

FIGURE 2

FIGURE 3

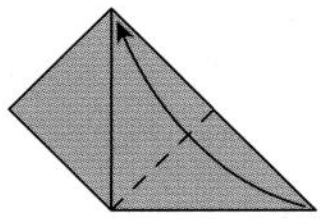

FIGURE 4

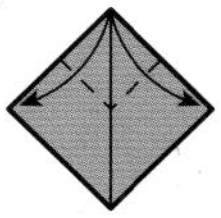

FIGURE 5

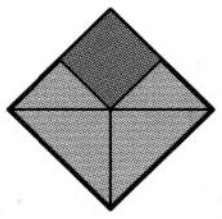

FIGURE 6

Musical Notes

This eye-catching card in black and orange is a favorite with music lovers. Notice how the embroidery is set into the angles formed by the folded teabag squares.

1. **CUT THE PAPERS:** From the black cardstock, cut a 4¾-inch square for the work piece. From the orange cardstock, cut a 5-inch square. From the ivory cardstock, cut a rectangle 5¼ x 10½ inches for the base card.

2. Score and fold the ivory base card (page 16) in half to form a 5¼-inch square.

3. Following the instructions in Getting Started (page 13), transfer the embroidery pattern to the black work piece, making the necessary perforations.

YOU'LL NEED

PAPERS

Cardstock: black, light orange, ivory, or colors to match the teabag paper (8½ x 11-inch sheets)

Teabag folding paper with printed music notes or design of your choice (five 1½-inch squares)

EMBELLISHMENTS

Gold metallic thread

Copper metallic thread

SUPPLIES

Hand-sewing needle

Removable tape

Double-sided tape

Glue stick

Scissors

Pencil

Paper cutter or craft knife and metal ruler

Craft foam (12 x 18-inch sheet)

Perforating tool

Scoring tool and bone paper folder (optional)

4. **EMBROIDER THE PATTERN:** With the pattern markings to guide you, stitch the center design. Using the gold metallic thread, stitch one section at a time: Come out at hole 9 of the left row of parallel rows of perforations and go into hole 1 of the opposite row. Continue stitching from one side to the other in ascending order on the left row and descending order on the right row, in the following sequence: 2 – 8, 7 – 3, 4 – 6, 5 – 5, 6 – 4, 3 – 7, 8 – 2 and 1 – 9. Complete each of the four sections in the same manner.

5. Using the copper metallic thread, stitch each outside corner: Come out hole 1 and go into hole 12. Continue stitching the corner shape in the following sequence: 13 – 2, 3 – 14, 15 – 4, 5 – 16, 17 – 6, 7 – 18, 19 – 8, 9 – 20, 21 – 10, 11 – 22, 23 – 12, 13 – 24, 25 – 14, 15 – 26, 27 – 16, 17 – 28, 29 – 18, 19 – 30, 31 – 20, 21 – 32, 1 – 22. Complete each of the four corners in the same manner.

6. Using the gold metallic thread, stitch from hole 23 of one corner to hole 11 of the next corner on each side to form the outline that will be the guideline for gluing the teabag papers.

7. Review Before You Begin at the start of this chapter.

8. **CUT THE TEABAG PAPERS:** Fold four of the teabag squares in half horizontally, making sure the design is facing the same direction before folding. Cut each of the four squares in half along the crease. You should have eight halves to work with. From the fifth square, choose the portion of the design that is most interesting and cut a ¾-inch square that includes it. Glue this square to the work piece in the center of the gold stitching.

9. **MAKE THE TEABAG FOLDS:** With the white (unprinted) side of the paper facing up, fold one of the eight teabag paper halves in half widthwise; unfold (figure 1). Next, fold the left side of the paper down to the center crease and fold the right side up to the center crease, forming a parallelogram (figure 2). Then fold the paper in half along the first crease you made (figure 3). Repeat to fold the remaining seven teabag paper halves, making sure the design is facing in the same direction on each half. Trim off any excess white paper showing on the completed folded shapes.

10. **PLACE THE TEABAG DESIGN:** Using the gold outline stitch made in step 6 as a guide, glue two folded teabag papers to each side of the work piece, aligned with the stitching pattern, as shown. Be aware of the different portions of the pattern on each folded paper and try to keep similar designs together.

11. Center and mount the completed work piece (page 16) onto the orange cardstock square using double-sided tape. To finish, similarly center and mount all layers onto the front of the base card.

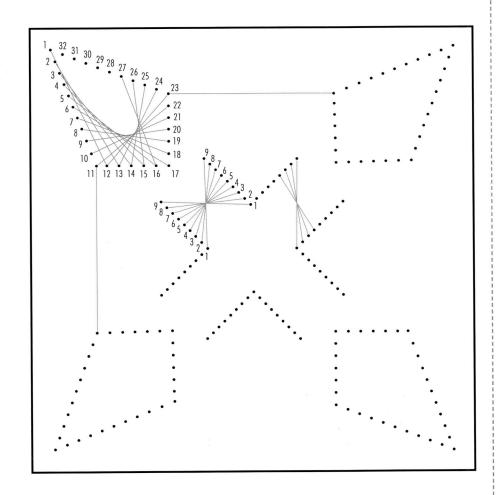

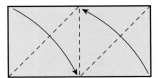

FIGURE 1

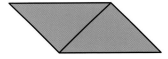

FIGURE 2

FIGURE 3

4

Iris Folding

BEFORE YOU BEGIN

Iris folding is another beautiful paper folding technique that originated in The Netherlands. For this usage, the term "iris" refers to the iris of your eye, which is like the shutter of a camera. When the shutter closes, the sides fold over each other, forming an overlapping spiral. In iris folding, overlying strips of folded lightweight paper are placed sequentially on a pattern that is taped to a cutout shape. The resulting design on the completed card is a spiraling image of that shape, although sometimes the folded strips are simply overlapped to create a fanlike or woven effect, as with the Seashell and Spring Leaf patterns (pages 80 and 82).

For the best results when iris folding, use lightweight papers such as origami, chiyogami, tissue paper, gift wrap, or foils. Heavier papers will create a bulge in the card as the strips are laid on top of each other. Ribbons can be used instead of paper strips in any iris folding project, as they were for the Lily and Christmas Bell cards (pages 91 and 96). Select ribbons that are ⅜ inch (9mm) wide and opaque enough so the tape securing the ribbon strips doesn't show through on the finished side.

Each project in this chapter comes with a pattern drawn for the specific shape used on the card. In the first two projects, Seashell (page 80) and Spring Leaf (page 82), the strips of paper are layered so that only the folded edge of the paper strips are visible and the spiraling doesn't occur. The remaining projects use the more traditional spiraling iris folding patterns. Photocopy the patterns in the chapter and place the strips directly over them, then tape the strips to the back of the cardstock (See Getting Started, page 14).

Begin each project by cutting strips of paper in the amount and colors required. Each strip will then be folded in half to create a folded edge that runs along the entire piece (Kaleidoscope cards, pages 140–157, use the same folded strips). If the work piece includes embroidery, transfer the necessary perforations onto the cardstock before stitching, because it will be difficult to do so after the layers are in place. Prior to embroidering, use the perforations as a guide to help you position the iris folding pattern. Once the shape is cut out, complete all the stitching before moving on to the next step.

There are many dye-cut stencils and templates available for cutting out shapes from cardstock. To cut out most of the shapes in this chapter, Fiskars® ShapeCutter™ and ShapeTemplate™ tools are suggested because they are readily available, inexpensive, and simple to use. But a stencil or template and a cutting tool would also work. If you have a stencil or template in a size larger or smaller than that used for your chosen project, adjust the pattern slightly. Add an additional layer of strips to the outside of the pattern if your stencil is larger or begin farther in the pattern if your stencil is smaller.

Begin the iris folding by centering the cutout portion of the work piece over the pattern provided. Place a small piece of removable tape on each side of the cardstock to prevent it from shifting. Each pattern has numbered sections that indicate where and the order in which the paper strips are to be placed. Be aware that the completed iris design, which is displayed on the right side of the work piece, is a mirror image of the drawn pattern.

The number of different colored paper strips required is based on how many strips are needed to complete one layer on the pattern's periphery. For example, the Kimono (page 88) pattern uses four paper strips to complete sections 1–4, which form the outermost layer of the square pattern. If the pattern calls for four or more different colored strips to be used, it's okay to repeat one or two of the colors. On the Kimono pattern only two colors were used, each repeated twice.

It's important to use the same color sequence for each layer placed on the pattern, whether the pattern calls for them to be placed clockwise or counterclockwise. For example, on the Japanese Fans (page 84) pattern three colors are used to complete the pattern. A gold strip is placed in section 1, a red strip in section 2, and a patterned strip in section 3, completing the first layer of the pattern. The next layer begins again with gold, this time placed in section 4, red in section 5, and a patterned strip in section 6. The subsequent layers of the pattern are laid down by continuing in this counterclockwise fashion, working toward the center, until the pattern is completed. To help you remember the sequence, place the colored strips on the table in the order they appear on the pattern.

Place the folded edge of each strip flush to the line marking the numbered section on the pattern. Trim the strip so the portion of it covering the numbered section is ⅛–¼ inch longer on each end than the section itself. Tape the ends to the back of the work piece with small pieces of transparent tape. Use the remainder of the strip for the subsequent sections requiring that color, trimming and taping it in the same manner. When you finish with one strip, begin with the next. Repeat this process to place the strips of different colors on the pattern. Remember to follow the same color sequence for each layer. Don't worry how this side of the work piece looks. The beautiful pattern will appear when all the strips have been placed, the pattern removed, and the work piece turned over.

If you lose your place while laying the strips on the pattern, look for the lowest number showing on the pattern and place the next strip there. Once all the numbered sections are filled, the center of the pattern will be left open. You may choose either to leave it that way, allowing the cardstock placed behind it to show through, or to tape one of the strips over the hole to fill in the pattern. Remove the work piece from the pattern, turn it over, and layer it along with other cardstock onto the base card as directed for each project.

Seashell

With the favorite children's tongue twister "She sells seashells by the seashore" as its inspiration, this first iris folding project is a good introduction to laying the folded edge of the paper strips flush to the lines of each numbered section.

YOU'LL NEED

PAPERS

Cardstock: bronze, ivory (8½ x 11-inch sheets)

Metallic bronze/blue marbled paper (8½ x 11-inch sheet)

Scraps of decorative papers in the following colors: gold foil, gold/ivory, black/gold origami paper

EMBELLISHMENT

Gold gel pen

SUPPLIES

Fiskars® ShapeCutter™ and Vacation ShapeTemplate™ with shell shape

Decorative corner punch

Tapes: removable, transparent, double-sided

Scissors

Pencil

Paper cutter or craft knife and metal ruler

Craft foam (12 x 18-inch sheet)

Scoring tool and bone paper folder (optional)

1. **CUT THE PAPERS:** From the bronze cardstock, cut a 4¾-inch square for the work piece. From the ivory cardstock, cut a rectangle 5¼ x 10½ inches for the base card. From the bronze/blue marbled paper, cut a 5-inch square and one ¾ x 4-inch strip. From the gold foil, cut a 1½-inch square and one ¾ x 4-inch strip. From the remaining scraps of decorative papers, cut one ¾ x 4-inch strip each. There should be a total of four strips.

2. Score and fold the ivory base card (page 16) in half to form a 5¼-inch square.

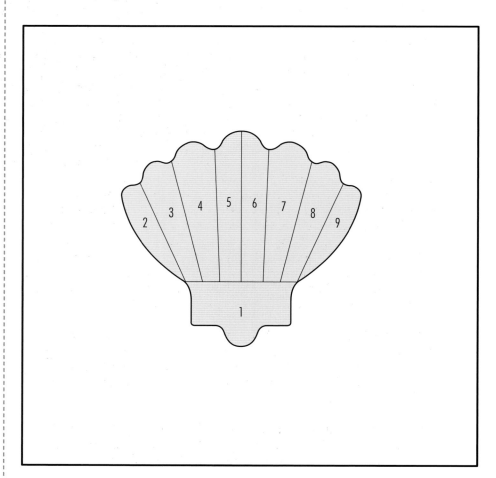

3. Review Before You Begin at the start of this chapter.

4. **PREPARE THE WORK PIECE:** Using the ShapeCutter™ and shell template, follow the manufacturer's instructions to cut out the shell from the center of the wrong side of the work piece. Center the work piece wrong side up over the shell pattern. Secure it in place with removable tape.

5. **FOLD AND LAYER THE STRIPS:** With the white (unprinted) side of the paper face up, fold in one edge of the small gold square. It does not need to be folded in half. With the printed side down, place the folded edge over section 1 of the pattern, making sure it is flush to the line. Tape it in place to the work piece, using transparent tape at each end.

6. With the white (unprinted) side of the paper face up, fold all the strips in half. Place them in the following sequence on the pattern, folded edge flush to the line: the bronze/blue strip in section 2, the gold/ivory strip in section 3, the origami strip in section 4, and the gold foil strip in section 5. As each color strip is placed, trim it so the portion covering the numbered section is about ¼ inch longer on each end than the section itself. Tape the ends to the work piece, using transparent tape. Repeat this color sequence for sections 6–9.

7. **COMPLETE THE WORK PIECE:** When all strips are in position, remove the work piece from the pattern and turn it right side up. Using the gold gel pen, write the words *She sells seashells* underneath the shell, if desired. Use the corner punch to make decorative corners on the work piece.

8. Center and mount the completed work piece (page 16) onto the bronze/blue marbled paper using double-sided tape. Similarly center and mount these layers onto the front of the base card.

Spring Leaf

This card is just right for sending springtime greetings. The alternating strips of soft green and gold paper are placed so that they form a simple woven pattern that suggests the unfurling of a brand-new leaf.

YOU'LL NEED

PAPERS

Cardstock: white, green pearl, gold pearl (8½ x 11-inch sheets)

Vellum in green-and-yellow leaf pattern

Tissue paper: gold pearl, green pearl

SUPPLIES

Fiskars® ShapeCutter™ and Leaves ShapeTemplate™ with mulberry leaf

Tapes: removable, transparent, double-sided

Scissors

Pencil

Paper cutter or craft knife and metal ruler

Craft foam (12 x 18-inch sheet)

Scoring tool and bone paper folder (optional)

1. **CUT THE PAPERS:** From the white card stock, cut a rectangle 4 x 6 inches. From the green pearl cardstock, cut a rectangle 4½ x 6½ inches. From the gold pearl cardstock cut a rectangle 6¾ x 9½

inches for the base card. From the vellum, cut a rectangle 4 x 6 inches. From the gold pearl tissue paper, cut a 1¼-inch square and two ¾ x 5-inch strips. From the green pearl tissue paper, cut two ¾ x 5-inch strips. There should be a total of four strips.

2. Using double-sided tape, mount the vellum onto the white rectangle, aligning the edges. This forms the work piece.

3. Score and fold the gold pearl base card (page 16) in half to form a rectangle 4¾ x 6¾ inches.

4. Review Before You Begin at the start of this chapter.

5. **PREPARE THE WORK PIECE:** Using the ShapeCutter™ and mulberry leaf template, follow the manufacturer's instructions to cut out the leaf from the center of the wrong side of the work piece. Work slowly as you cut out the work piece as vellum can tear easily. Center the work piece wrong side up over the leaf pattern. Secure it in place with removable tape.

6. **FOLD AND LAYER THE STRIPS:** With the white (unprinted) side of the tissue paper face up, fold in one edge of the small gold pearl square. It does not need to be folded in half. With the printed side down, place the folded edge over section A of the pattern, making sure it is flush to the line at section 1. Tape it in place to the work piece, using transparent tape at each end.

7. With the white side of the tissue paper face up, fold all the strips in half. Place the first layer of strips in the following sequence on the pattern, folded edge flush to the line: the green pearl strip in section 1, the gold pearl in section 2. As each color strip is placed, trim it so the portion covering the numbered section is about ¼ inch longer on each end than the section itself. Tape the ends to the work piece using transparent tape. Repeat this color sequence following the numerical order on the pattern until the strips fill the pattern. Remove the work piece from the pattern and turn it right side up.

8. Center and mount the completed work piece (page 16) onto the green pearl rectangle using double-sided tape. To finish, similarly center and mount these layers onto the front of the base card.

Japanese Fans

This striking card was inspired by the fans used by Japanese Kabuki dancers. It takes full advantage of the beautifully patterned chiyogami paper. The gold tassel and folded fans make the three-dimensional design leap off the page.

YOU'LL NEED

PAPERS

Cardstock: black, red (8½ x 11-inch sheets)

Gold foil paper (8½ x 11-inch sheet)

Red foil paper

Chiyogami paper with a black/gold/red/blue/green design

EMBELLISHMENT

Braided gold metallic thread

SUPPLIES

Fiskars® ShapeCutter™ and Diamonds and Circles ShapeTemplates™

Craft glue

Tapes: removable, transparent, double-sided

Scissors

Pencil

Paper cutter or craft knife and metal ruler

Craft foam (12 x 18-inch sheet)

Scoring tool and bone paper folder (optional)

1. **CUT THE PAPERS:** From the black cardstock, cut a rectangle 5 x 6 inches for the work piece. From the red cardstock, cut a rectangle 6½ x 11 inches for the base card and two 1½-inch squares. From the gold foil, cut a rectangle 5¼ x 6¼ inches and two ¾ x 8-inch strips. From the red foil, cut two ¾ x 8-inch strips. From the chiyogami paper, cut two rectangles 1½ x 3 inches, one rectangle 1¾ x 2¼ inches, and two ¾ x 8-inch strips. There should be a total of six strips.

2. Score and fold the red base card (page 16) in half to form a rectangle 5½ x 6½ inches.

3. Review Before You Begin at the start of this chapter.

4. **PREPARE THE WORK PIECE:** To make the fan shape, place the bottom half of the 2½ x 4¾-inch diamond template on the wrong side of the work piece, to the right of the center of the card, and outline the half-diamond. Align a portion of the circumference of the 3½-inch circle template with the sides of the open end of the half-diamond. Outline that portion of the circle to connect the sides, creating the fan shape. Cut out the fan with the ShapeCutter™ following the manufacturer's instructions; neaten the top corners with the craft knife if necessary. Center the work piece wrong side up over the fan pattern. Secure it in place with removable tape.

5. **FOLD AND LAYER THE STRIPS:** With the white (unprinted) side of the paper face up, fold all the strips in half and separate them into piles according to color. Place the first layer of strips on the pattern in the following sequence, folded edge flush to the line: the gold foil in section 1, the red foil in section 2, the chiyogami paper in section 3. As each color strip is placed, trim it so the portion covering the numbered section is about ¼ inch longer on each end than the section itself. Tape the ends to the work piece, using transparent tape. Repeat this color sequence following the numerical order on the pattern until the strips fill the pattern. Tape a piece of the chiyogami paper over the center hole. Remove the work piece from the pattern and turn it right side up.

6. **COMPLETE THE WORK PIECE:** With the photograph as a guide, affix the two small red squares on point along the right edge of the work piece, equidistant apart, using double-sided tape. Fold the two 1½ x 3-inch chiyogami rectangles accordion-style to make two fans. Tie the bottom of each fan with a piece of gold thread to keep it in place. Glue one fan to each of the small red squares. If desired, cut a small piece from the bottom left corner of the work piece and place the 1¾ x 2¼-inch chiyogami rectangle behind it. Trim the corner piece, and glue it back in position, leaving a small strip of the chiyogami paper showing.

7. **MAKE THE TASSEL:** Cut a 2-foot length of the gold thread and wrap it around your hand. Remove it from your hand and wrap a small piece of gold thread around the loops at one end, about ½ inch from the top; tie a knot. Cut all the bottom loops to form the tassel. Glue the tassel to the bottom of the fan.

8. Center and mount the completed work piece (page 16) onto the gold foil rectangle using double-sided tape. To finish, similarly mount these layers onto the front of the base card.

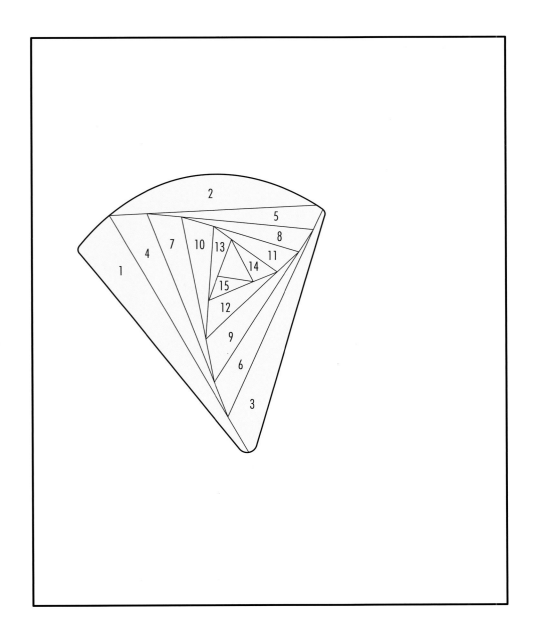

Kimono

Embroidery, iris folding, and napkin cutouts each lend its distinctive decorative appeal to this beautiful card. Focusing on a theme and using just a few vibrant colors unites the different elements.

YOU'LL NEED

PAPERS

Cardstock: black, gold pearl, red (8½ x 11-inch sheets)

Chiyogami paper with Chinese characters: red with gold, gold with black

Printed paper napkin or decorative paper with Chinese symbols

Small piece of adhesive-backed paper (2 x 3 inches; to use with napkin only)

EMBELLISHMENTS

Gold metallic thread #4 braid

Rust metallic thread #4 braid

SUPPLIES

Fiskars® ShapeCutter™ and Squares ShapeTemplate™ or template for 2-inch square and cutting tool

Hand-sewing needle

Tapes: removable, transparent, double-sided

Glue stick

Scissors

Pencil

Paper cutter or craft knife and metal ruler

Craft foam (12 x 18-inch sheet)

Perforating tool

Scoring tool and bone paper folder (optional)

1. **CUT THE PAPERS:** From the black cardstock, cut a 5-inch square for the work piece. From the gold pearl cardstock, cut a 5¼-inch square. From the red cardstock, cut a rectangle 5½ x 11 inches for the base card. From each of the chiyogami papers, cut three ¾ x 8-inch strips. There should be a total of six strips. From the napkin or decorative paper, cut three symbols, 1–1¼ inches each.

2. Score and fold the red base card (page 16) in half to form a 5½-inch square.

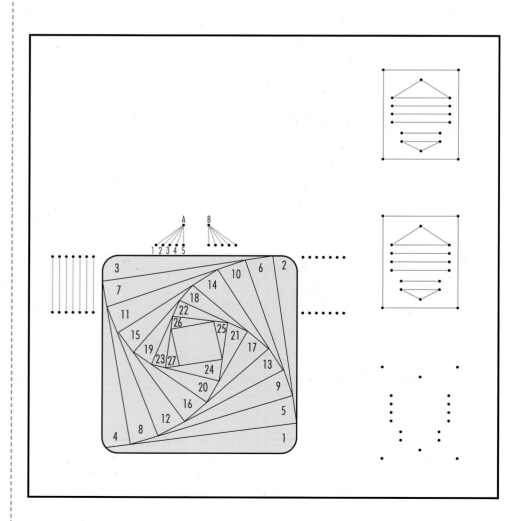

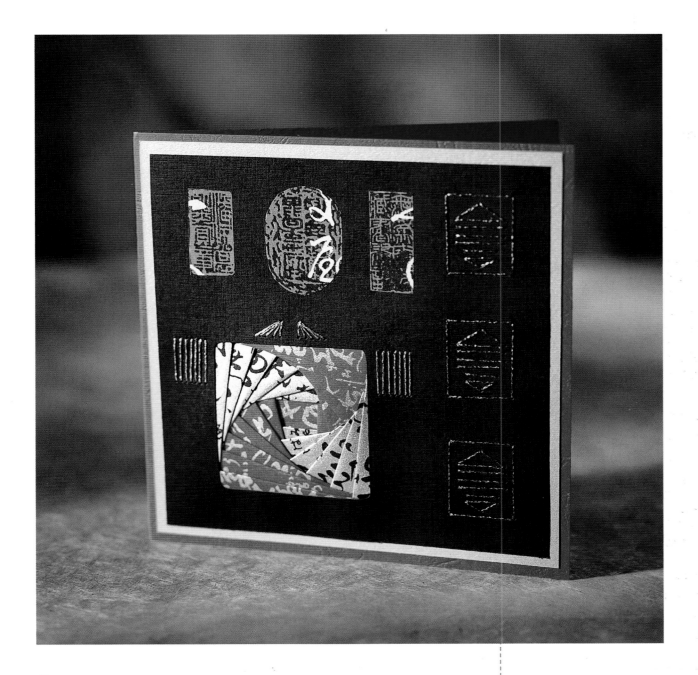

3. Following the instructions in Getting Started (page 13), transfer the embroidery pattern to the black work piece, making the necessary perforations.

4. Review Before You Begin at the start of this chapter.

5. **PREPARE THE WORK PIECE:** Using the perforations as a guide and the ShapeCutter™ and 2-inch square template, follow the manufacturer's instructions to cut out the square from the center of the

wrong side of the work piece. Be sure the top of the square is equidistant from both sleeves of the kimono and the collar. (If using a template and cutting tool, cut along the lines of the square to remove it from the work piece.)

6. **EMBROIDER THE PATTERN:** With the pattern markings to guide you, stitch the kimono using the gold metallic thread. Each sleeve is embroidered using seven large straight stitches, working from left to right. The collar is stitched by coming out at hole A and stitching into holes 1–5 on the left-hand side, always returning to A to begin each new stitch. Then come out at hole B and stitch in the same manner on the right-hand side.

7. Using the rust metallic thread, stitch the three rectangles with Chinese symbols, working from the top down. Stitch the outline of the rectangles first, then the interior symbols: a triangle, four horizontal lines, and a smaller triangle.

8. **MAKE THE NAPKIN DECORATIONS:** If using a paper napkin, read Before You Begin at the start of chapter 5. Discard all but the printed layer of the three cutout napkin symbols. Peel the backing from the adhesive-backed paper and place the symbols on it; cut out the three symbols. Using the photo as a guide, glue the symbols onto the top of the card, spacing them evenly. If using symbols cut from decorative paper, trim them neatly before gluing.

9. **FOLD AND LAYER THE STRIPS:** Center the embroidered work piece wrong side up over the pattern. Secure it in place with removable tape. With the white (unprinted) side of the chiyogami paper face up, fold the strips in half and separate them into piles according to color.

10. Place the first layer of strips on the pattern in the following sequence, folded edge flush to the line: the red/gold in section 1, the gold/black in section 2, the red/gold in section 3, the gold/black in section 4. As each color strip is placed, trim it so the portion covering the numbered section is about ¼ inch longer on each end than the section itself. Tape the ends to the work piece, using transparent tape. Continue alternating colors following the numerical order on the pattern until the strips fill the pattern. Tape a piece of red/gold chiyogami paper over the center hole. Remove the work piece from the pattern and turn it right side up.

11. Center and mount the completed work piece (page 16) onto the gold pearl square using double-sided tape. To finish, similarly mount these layers onto the front of the base card.

Lily

Hand-dyed silk ribbons, instead of folded paper strips, and a delicate touch of embroidery add a sophistication and rich depth of color to this floral card.

1. **CUT THE CARDSTOCK:** From the black, cut a 4¾-inch square for the work piece. From the red, cut a 4¾-inch square. From the blue pearl, cut a 5-inch square. From the light blue, cut a rectangle 5¼ x 10½ inches for the base card.

2. Score and fold the light blue base card (page 16) in half to form a 5¼-inch square.

3. Following the instructions in Getting Started (page 13), transfer the embroidery pattern to the black work piece, making the necessary perforations.

4. Review Before You Begin at the start of this chapter.

5. **PREPARE THE WORK PIECE:** Using the perforations as a guide, and the ShapeCutter™ and petal template, follow the manufacturer's instructions to cut out the petal from the wrong side of the work piece, directly below the top end of the perforated stem.

6. **EMBROIDER THE PATTERN:** With the pattern markings to guide you, stitch the leaves and stem of the flower. Using the light green metallic thread, stitch the leaves: Come out hole A and stitch into holes 1–7 of the leaf, always returning to A to start each new stitch. Similarly stitch the leaves originating from holes B and C. Using the antique gold metallic thread, stitch the stem: Beginning at the left end of the stem, backstitch along the entire stem until you reach the flower.

7. **LAYER THE RIBBON STRIPS:** Center the work piece wrong side up over the pattern. Secure it in place with removable tape. Using the full length of the ribbons, place them in sequence on the pattern, edge flush to the line: the blue in section 1, the orange in section 2, and the purple in section 3. As each color ribbon is placed, trim it so the portion covering the numbered section is about ¼ inch longer on each end than the section itself. As ribbon may have some give, make sure to pull it taut to lay flat on the pattern. Tape the ends to the work piece using transparent tape. (If the ribbon is very delicate, place extra tape over the ends to give them support.) Repeat this color sequence, following the numerical order on the pattern, until the ribbon strips fill the pattern. Tape a piece of orange ribbon over the center hole.

YOU'LL NEED

PAPERS

Cardstock: black, red, blue pearl, light blue (8½ x 11-inch sheets)

EMBELLISHMENTS

Light green metallic thread

Antique gold metallic thread #4 braid

⅜-inch-wide silk ombré ribbon: blue, purple, orange (1 yard each)

SUPPLIES

Fiskars® ShapeCutter™ and Flowers ShapeTemplate™ with petal shape

Decorative corner punch

Hand-sewing needle

Tapes: removable, transparent, double-sided

Scissors

Pencil

Paper cutter or craft knife and metal ruler

Craft foam (12 x 18-inch sheet)

Perforating tool

Scoring tool and bone paper folder (optional)

8. **COMPLETE THE WORK PIECE:** When all strips are in position, remove the work piece from the pattern and turn it right side up. Use the punch to make decorative corners.

9. Using double-sided tape, mount the completed work piece (page 16) onto the red square, aligning the edges. Center and mount these layers onto the blue pearl square using double-sided tape. To finish, similarly center and mount all layers onto the front of the base card.

Oval Ornament

With its festive mix of folded foil paper and holiday wrapping paper, this Christmas ornament card may eventually be found hanging on the recipient's tree as a real ornament.

YOU'LL NEED

PAPERS

Cardstock: black, tan (8½ x 11-inch sheets)

Copper foil paper (8½ x 11-inch sheet)

Scrap of gold foil

Red/gold tissue paper

Red/green decorative paper

SUPPLIES

Fiskars® ShapeCutter™ and Flowers and Christmas ShapeTemplates™ with leaf and ornament hook

Tapes: removable, transparent, double-sided

Scissors

Pencil

Paper cutter or craft knife and metal ruler

Craft foam (12 x 18-inch sheet)

Scoring tool and bone paper folder (optional)

1. **CUT THE PAPERS:** From the black cardstock, cut a rectangle 4½ x 5¼ inches for the work piece. From the tan cardstock, cut a rectangle 5¾ x 10 inches for the base card. From the copper foil, cut a rectangle 4¾ x 5½ inches and three ¾ x 8-inch strips. From the gold foil, cut a 1-inch square. From the tissue paper and decorative paper, cut two ¾ x 8-inch strips each. There should be a total of seven strips.

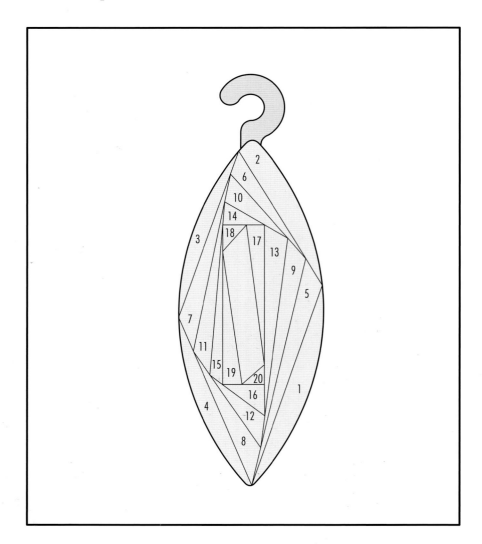

2. Score and fold the tan base card (page 16) in half to form a rectangle 5 x 5¾ inches.

3. Review Before You Begin at the start of this chapter.

4. **PREPARE THE WORK PIECE:** Using the ShapeCutter™ and the leaf shape on the template, follow the manufacturer's instructions to cut out the leaf from the center of the wrong side of the work piece. Do the same with the top portion of the hook on the Christmas template, centering it onto the top of the leaf-shaped ornament. Center the work piece wrong side up over the ornament pattern. Secure it in place with removable tape.

5. **FOLD AND LAYER THE STRIPS:** With the white (unprinted) side of the paper face up, fold in one edge of the gold square. It does not need to be folded in half. With the printed side down, place the folded edge over the hook area of the pattern, making sure it is flush to the line separating the hook from the ornament. Tape it in place to the work piece using transparent tape at each end.

6. With the white side of the paper face up, fold all the strips in half and separate them into piles according to color. Place the first layer of strips on the pattern in the following sequence, folded edge flush to the line: the red/gold tissue in section 1, the copper foil in section 2, the red/green paper in section 3, and the copper foil in section 4. As each color strip is placed, trim it so the portion covering the numbered section is about ¼ inch longer on each end than the section itself. Tape the ends in place to the work piece, using transparent tape. Repeat this color sequence following the numerical order on the pattern until the strips fill the pattern. Tape a piece of the copper foil over the center hole. Remove the work piece from the pattern and turn it right side up.

7. Center and mount the completed work piece (see page 16) onto the copper foil rectangle using double-sided tape. To finish, similarly center and mount these layers onto the front of the base card.

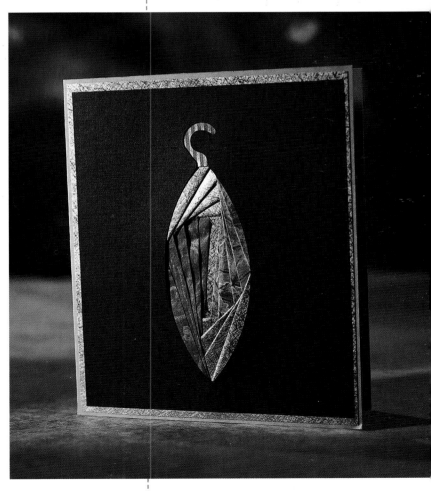

Christmas Bell

On this holiday card, swirling bands of colorful silk ribbons are strategically placed to enhance the bell's shape and give it added dimension.

YOU'LL NEED

PAPERS

Cardstock: red, gold pearl
(8½ x 11-inch sheets)

Forest green handmade paper
(8½ x 11-inch sheet)

EMBELLISHMENTS

⅜-inch-wide silk ombré ribbon: burgundy, yellow, green, burgundy stripe (about 2 feet each)

⅜-inch-wide gold metallic ribbon (6 inches)

SUPPLIES

Fiskars® ShapeCutter™ and School ShapeTemplate™ with bell

Tapes: removable, transparent, double-sided

Scissors

Pencil

Paper cutter or craft knife and metal ruler

Craft foam (12 x 18-inch sheet)

Scoring tool and bone paper folder (optional)

1. **CUT THE PAPERS:** From the red cardstock, cut a rectangle 3¾ x 5 inches for the work piece. From the gold pearl cardstock, cut a rectangle 6 x 10 inches for the base card. From the handmade green paper, cut a rectangle 4½ x 5¾ inches.

2. Score and fold the gold pearl base card (page 16) in half to form a rectangle 5 x 6 inches.

3. Review Before You Begin at the start of this chapter.

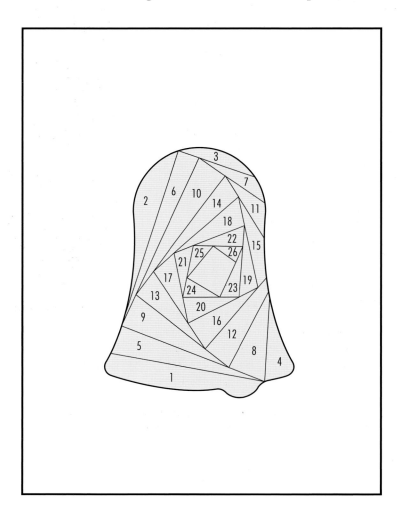

4. **PREPARE THE WORK PIECE:** Using the ShapeCutter™ and the bell shape on the template, follow the manufacturer's instructions to cut out the bell from the center of the wrong side of the work piece. Center the work piece wrong side up over the pattern. Secure it in place with removable tape.

5. **LAYER THE RIBBON STRIPS:** Using the full length of the ribbons, place the first layer of strips on the pattern in the following sequence, edge flush to the line: the burgundy ribbon in section 1, the yellow in section 2, the green in section 3, and the burgundy stripe in section 4. As each color ribbon is placed, trim it so the portion covering the numbered section is about ¼ inch longer on each end than the section itself. As ribbon may have some give, make sure to pull it taut to lay flat on the pattern. Tape the ends to the work piece using transparent tape. (If the ribbon is very delicate, place extra tape over the ends to give them support.) Repeat this color sequence following the numerical order on the pattern until the ribbon strips fill the pattern. Tape a piece of green ribbon over the center hole. Remove the work piece from the pattern and turn it right side up.

6. Center and mount the completed work piece (page 16) onto the handmade green paper rectangle using double-sided tape. Similarly center and mount these layers onto the front of the base card.

7. To finish, make a bow from the gold metallic ribbon and attach it to the top of the bell using double-sided tape.

Antique Star

The embroidered eight-pointed star on this card resembles an antique filigree brooch, and the small silver-and-white iris-folded square in the center suggests a glittery gem or cut crystal.

YOU'LL NEED

PAPERS

Cardstock: dark blue, light blue sparkle, robin's-egg blue, and white sparkle (8½ x 11-inch sheets)

Tissue paper: scrap each of silver/white patterned and silver

EMBELLISHMENT

Antique silver twist metallic thread

SUPPLIES

Fiskars® ShapeCutter™ and Squares ShapeTemplates™ or template for ¾-inch square and cutting tool

Decorative corner punch

Hand-sewing needle

Tapes: removable, transparent, double-sided

Scissors

Pencil

Paper cutter or craft knife with metal ruler

Perforating tool

Scoring tool and bone paper folder (optional)

1. **CUT THE PAPERS:** From the dark blue cardstock, cut a 4¼-inch square for the work piece. From the light blue sparkle cardstock, cut a 4¼-inch square. From the robin's-egg blue cardstock, cut a 3¾-inch square. From the white sparkle cardstock, cut a rectangle 5½ x 11 inches for the base card. From each color tissue paper cut one ¾ x 4-inch strip. There should be a total of two strips.

2. Score and fold the white sparkle base card (page 16) in half to form a 5½-inch square.

3. Following the instructions in Getting Started (page 13), transfer the embroidery pattern to the dark blue work piece, making the necessary perforations.

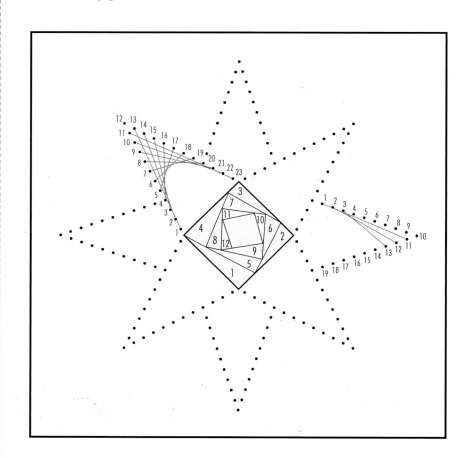

4. Review Before You Begin at the start of this chapter.

5. **PREPARE THE WORK PIECE:** Using the perforations as a guide, and the ShapeCutter™ and ¾-inch square template, follow the manufacturer's instructions to cut out the square from the center of the star on the wrong side of the work piece. (If using a template and cutting tool, cut along the lines of the square to remove it from the work piece.) Turn the work piece right side up.

6. **EMBROIDER THE PATTERN:** With the pattern markings to guide you, stitch the star using the silver twist thread. There are four small points and four large points on the star. Come out at hole 1 on a large point and go into hole 13. Continue stitching in the following sequence: hole 14 – 2, 3 – 15, 16 – 4, 5 – 17, 18 – 6, 7 – 19, 20 – 8, 9 – 21, 22 – 10, 11 – 23. Outline the large star point by coming out at the bottom hole on both sides and into the unused hole on the top. Carry the thread to the closest small point and stitch it by coming out at hole 1 and going into hole 11. Continue stitching in the following sequence: 12 – 2, 3 – 13, 14 – 4, 5 – 15, 16 – 6, 7 – 17, 18 – 8, 9 – 19. Outline the small point as you did the large one. Repeat stitching, alternating large and small star points, until the embroidery is completed.

7. **FOLD AND LAYER THE STRIPS:** Center the embroidered work piece wrong side up over the pattern. Secure it in place with removable tape. With the white (unprinted) side of the paper face up, fold the tissue paper strips in half. Place the first layer of strips on the pattern in the following sequence, folded edge flush to the line: the silver/white patterned tissue in section 1, the silver tissue in section 2. As each color strip is placed, trim it so the portion covering the numbered section is about ¼ inch longer on each end than the section itself. Tape the ends to the work piece, using transparent tape. Repeat this color sequence following the numerical order on the pattern until the strips fill the pattern. Tape a piece of the silver/white tissue over the center hole.

8. **COMPLETE THE WORK PIECE:** When all strips are in position, remove the work piece from the pattern and turn it right side up. Use the punch to make decorative corners.

9. Using double-sided tape, mount the completed work piece (page 16) onto the light blue sparkle square, aligning edges. Center and mount the robin's-egg blue square on point to the front of the base card. To finish, center and mount the layered work piece onto the robin's-egg blue square as shown, using double-sided tape.

5

Napkin Cutouts

BEFORE YOU BEGIN

Paper napkins have a lot to recommend them to makers of handmade greeting cards. They add a soft, almost tissuelike texture to the cards. They also offer a huge range of designs to suit everyone's taste and any occasion, and they can be purchased almost anywhere paper goods are sold.

Rummage through your kitchen and you'll probably find decorative napkins you have put away from your last party or special event. You may even want to ask friends to swap or donate napkins so you can have a wider variety on hand from which to choose.

Before using a paper napkin for card making, you must first make it stronger so it can be cut and manipulated easily. Paper napkins usually are comprised of two or three layers, called plies, and are referred to as being either two- or three-ply. For card making, we work with only the printed layer and usually one quarter of a square napkin.

To prepare the napkin for use, open it to its full size, select the quadrant with the images you want to use, and cut along the folds with scissors to yield a smaller square. Then gently peel off the bottom two layers, leaving only the very fine top, printed, layer. Be careful not to rip the printed layer when separating the plies.

Next, reinforce the printed layer with adhesive-backed paper or self-adhesive labels. Both are available in 8½ x 11-inch sheets at office-supply stores. Cut the adhesive-backed paper to the size specified for the project. Peel the backing from the paper, and gently place it on the back of the napkin over the design you want to use. (You can also place the napkin face down on the work surface and place the adhesive-backed paper on it. Try both ways to see which works best.) Smooth the napkin onto the adhesive paper, using your fingers to get rid of any wrinkles. Most wrinkles will disappear if you keep rubbing over the same spot. Once the napkin is adhered to the adhesive paper, the reinforced images or small pieces required by the project can be cut out.

The projects in this chapter use paper napkins in a variety of ways to embellish the cards. A few are very simple, like the Blue Iris and Christmas Images (pages 105 and 108), in which large portions of the napkins are glued to the card in much the same way as any decorative paper. The three quiltlike cards (pages 120, 122, and 124) are designed as individual quilt blocks, combining small cut squares or triangles with embroidery. An inexpensive drafting template that has a series of squares in different sizes is a useful tool for these cards. Daisy Power, Bordered Butterfly, and Captured Hearts cards (pages 106, 111, and 118) use beads and embroidery to enhance the napkin designs. And the Pop-up Pansy and African Mask cards (pages 114 and 116) employ specific cutout shapes that are raised off the card surface on small foam adhesive squares and embellished with fibers. If the card you choose to make has embroidery, do that first, as the stitches will become guidelines for placing the napkin pieces.

Blue Iris

Using gold embossing powder to highlight areas of a napkin with a large floral design is an easy way to add sparkle and pizzazz to a simple image.

1. **CUT OUT THE PAPERS:** From the midnight blue cardstock, cut a rectangle 4¾ x 6½ inches. From the sage green cardstock, cut a strip 1¼ x 6¼ inches and a strip ¼ x 6¾ inches. From the white cardstock, cut a rectangle 7 x 10 inches for the base card. From the napkin, cut one quadrant with a large iris or other flower motif.

2. Score and fold the white base card (page 16) in half to form a rectangle 5 x 7 inches.

3. Review Before You Begin at the start of this chapter.

4. **PREPARE THE NAPKIN:** Separate the napkin layers and discard all but the printed top layer. Using a ruler or template, draw a rectangle 4½ x 6¼ inches onto the front of the adhesive-backed paper; cut it out. Select the portion of the floral image on the napkin you want to use. Remove the backing from the adhesive paper and place it adhesive side up on the work surface. Center the printed layer of the cut napkin on the adhesive and gently press it into position. Smooth the napkin with your fingers, rubbing gently to remove any wrinkles. Trim the excess napkin. Cut away the background surrounding the right of the floral image.

5. **CONSTRUCT THE WORK PIECE:** Using double-sided tape, affix the large sage green strip to the right edge of the midnight blue cardstock, leaving about ⅛-inch border of the midnight blue showing at the edge and about ¼ inch at the top and bottom. Position the napkin so that a border of about ⅛ inch of the midnight blue cardstock shows at the left edge and the top and bottom edges are aligned with the sage green cardstock. Glue the napkin to the midnight blue cardstock and to the left of the sage green strip.

6. Using the glue pen, outline the flowers and leaves on the napkin that you want highlighted. While the glue is still wet, sprinkle on the embossing powder; shake off excess. Use the heat gun to melt the embossing powder. As an alternative to embossing, outline the flowers and leaves with a glitter glue pen.

7. Glue the narrow sage green strip flush with the fold on the front of the base card. Center and mount the completed work piece (page 16) to the right of the green strip using double-sided tape.

YOU'LL NEED

PAPERS

Cardstock: midnight blue, sage green, white (8½ x 11-inch sheets)

Paper napkin with large iris print or any other large flower print

Adhesive-backed paper (8½ x 11-inch sheet)

EMBELLISHMENT

Gold embossing powder, glue pen, and craft heat gun; or gold glitter glue pen

SUPPLIES

Glue stick

Double-sided tape

Scissors

Pencil

Paper cutter or craft knife and metal ruler

Craft foam (12 x 18-inch sheet)

Scoring tool and bone paper folder (optional)

Daisy Power

A single flower cut from a floral print napkin is the basis for this bright and cheerful design. A few beads and backstitches lend texture and depth.

YOU'LL NEED

PAPERS

Cardstock: black, yellow, white (8½ x 11-inch sheets)

Paper napkin with large white daisy or other large flower

Adhesive-backed paper (8½ x 11-inch sheet)

EMBELLISHMENTS

Blue metallic thread

Large blue seed beads (at least 12)

SUPPLIES

Hand-sewing needle

Glue stick

Double-sided tape

Scissors

Pencil

Paper cutter or craft knife and metal ruler

Craft foam (12 x 18-inch sheet)

Perforating tool

Scoring tool and bone paper folder (optional)

1. **CUT THE PAPERS:** From the black cardstock, cut a rectangle 2¾ x 4¾ inches for the work piece. From the yellow cardstock, cut two 1½ x 6½-inch strips. From the white cardstock, cut a rectangle 6½ x 9½ inches for the base card. From the napkin, cut one quadrant with a large daisy or other flower.

2. Score and fold the white base card (page 16) in half to form a rectangle 4¾ x 6½ inches.

3. Review Before You Begin at the start of this chapter.

4. **PREPARE THE NAPKIN:** Separate the napkin layers and discard all but the printed top layer. Cut a rectangle 4½ x 5½ inches from the adhesive-backed paper; reserve the remainder for other projects. Remove the backing from the adhesive paper and place it adhesive side up on the work surface. Roughly cut a circle around the daisy. Place the rough-cut daisy on the adhesive and gently press it into position. Smooth the napkin with your fingers, rubbing gently to remove any wrinkles. Carefully cut around the petals to remove the background. Glue the reinforced cutout daisy onto the center of the black work piece.

5. **SEW ON BEADS:** Using the perforating tool, make holes around the yellow center of the flower, spacing them far enough apart to fit each bead. The size and type of the flower used will determine how many beads you can sew onto the center. Following the instructions for adding beads (page 15), sew the blue beads in place using the perforations and the blue metallic thread.

6. Select a few petals to highlight with the blue metallic thread. Using the perforating tool, make a few holes along one edge of the chosen petals. Using the blue metallic thread, backstitch along the edges of the petals to make them stand out.

7. Using double-sided tape, affix the two yellow strips to the front of the base card leaving a ½ inch space between them and at the top and bottom of the card. To finish, center and mount the completed work piece (page 16) over the yellow strips on the base card using double-sided tape.

TIP

Any paper napkin with a large floral design can be used for this project.
For those flowers without a center, embellish the card by highlighting
more petals in backstitches using a heavier-weight thread.

Christmas Images

Send your season's greetings on a card decorated with scenes cut from a Christmas-themed napkin and bordered by shining embroidery that represents that starry night in Bethlehem long ago.

YOU'LL NEED

PAPERS

Cardstock: dark blue and blue-gray sparkle (8½ x 11-inch sheets)

Metallic blue-gray decorative paper (8½ x 11-inch sheet)

Paper napkin with Christmas theme

Adhesive-backed paper (8½ x 11-inch sheet)

EMBELLISHMENTS

Blue metallic thread #4 braid

White sparkle blending filament

SUPPLIES

Hand-sewing needle

Glue stick

Removable tape

Double-sided tape

Scissors

Pencil

Paper cutter or craft knife and metal ruler

Craft foam (12 x 18-inch sheet)

Perforating tool

Scoring tool and bone paper folder (optional)

1. **CUT THE PAPERS:** From the dark blue cardstock, cut a rectangle 4 x 7 inches for the work piece. From the blue-gray sparkle cardstock, cut a rectangle 7½ x 9 inches for the base card. From the metallic blue-gray paper, cut a rectangle 4¼ x 7¼ inches. From the napkin, cut one quadrant (or more if needed) with Christmas images.

2. Score and fold the blue-gray sparkle base card (page 16) in half to form a rectangle 4½ x 7½ inches.

3. Following the instructions in Getting Started (page 13), transfer the embroidery pattern to the dark blue work piece, making the necessary perforations.

4. Review Before You Begin at the start of this chapter.

5. **EMBROIDER THE PATTERN:** With the pattern markings to guide you, and using the blue metallic thread, stitch the two sets of three horizontal lines, running along the top and bottom of the card. Complete one full row before moving on to the next, making sure to skip over the perforations made for the stars. Begin at the top left and stitch from left to right. Carry the thread down to the next row and stitch from right to left. Come up on the last row and stitch again from left to right. Carry the thread to the top right hole of the bottom set of lines and stitch from right to left. Stitch the next row from left to right, and the last row from right to left.

6. Using a doubled strand of the white sparkle blending filament, stitch each of the eight stars. Begin each star by coming out at the topmost hole and making a straight vertical stitch into the hole directly below it. Then stitch an X over the vertical line. Carry the thread over and continue to stitch each star in the same manner until all stars are completed. Be sure the X is crossed in the same direction on each star.

7. **PREPARE THE NAPKIN:** Separate the napkin layers and discard all but the printed top layer. Cut the sheet of adhesive-backed paper in half, reserving one half for another project. Remove the backing from the other half and place it face up on the work surface.

Center the printed layer of the cut napkin on the adhesive and gently press it into position. Smooth the napkin with your fingers, rubbing gently to remove any wrinkles. Select one, two, or three holiday scenes on the napkin you want to use. Cut out each scene, making sure to trim the pieces so they are 1¾ inches high or less and when placed together are no more than 6½ inches in length. Trim them slightly lengthwise so when they're positioned there will be about ¹⁄₁₆ inch between them. Glue the pieces centered between the two sets of stitching.

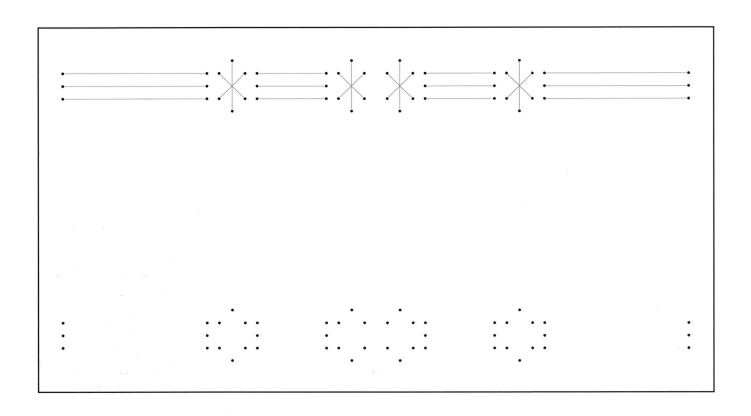

8. Center and mount the completed work piece (page 16) onto the metallic blue-gray paper rectangle using double-sided tape. To finish, similarly center and mount these layers onto the front of the base card.

VARIATION

Make the card vertical. Substitute traditional Christmas green and red cardstock for the dark blue cardstock and metallic blue-gray paper, and white cardstock for the base card. Cut a single 1¾ x 6½ -inch strip from a holiday-themed napkin. Do all embroidery using variegated gold/blue/pink metallic thread.

Bordered Butterfly

The striking floral border of a napkin is the focal point of this lovely card. The single butterfly, cut from the same napkin, is embellished with shimmering stitching and tiny beads.

1. **CUT THE PAPERS:** From the ivory pearl cardstock, cut a 4¾-inch square for the work piece. From the purple cardstock, cut a 5-inch square. From the mauve pearl cardstock, cut a rectangle 5¼ x 10½ inches for the base card. From the napkin(s), cut a quadrant with the border and a rough cut of the butterfly.

2. Score and fold the mauve pearl base card (page 16) in half to form a 5¼-inch square.

3. Review Before You Begin at the start of this chapter.

4. **PREPARE THE NAPKIN:** Separate the napkin layers and discard all but the printed top layer. Remove the backing from the adhesive paper and place it adhesive side up on the work surface. Place the printed layer of the napkin border and a rough cutout of the butterfly on the adhesive and gently press them into position. Smooth the napkin onto the adhesive paper with your fingers, rubbing gently to remove any wrinkles. Trim excess adhesive paper. Cut out a right angle of the border to the dimensions of the work piece; cut out the butterfly.

5. Glue the reinforced border into place along the left and top of the work piece, aligning the two papers. Center and glue the butterfly onto the work piece inside the border.

6. Using the perforating tool, make holes spaced about ⅛ inch apart outlining the butterfly wings. Make two holes on the head of the butterfly and another two holes about ¼ inch above each of them to form the antennae. Then make about five holes on each wing to add beads for embellishment.

7. **ADD EMBROIDERY AND BEADS:** Using the mauve metallic thread and the perforations made, backstitch along the butterfly wings. Next, make two straight stitches to form the antennae. Following the instructions for adding beads (page 15), and using the mauve metallic thread and beading needle, sew the mauve beads onto both wings and to the end of both antennae.

YOU'LL NEED

PAPERS

Cardstock: ivory pearl, purple, mauve pearl (8½ x 11-inch sheets)

Paper napkin with floral border and butterfly motif (or separate napkins for each design)

Adhesive-backed paper (8½ x 11-inch sheet)

EMBELLISHMENTS

Mauve metallic thread #4 braid

Metallic mauve seed beads (12)

SUPPLIES

Hand-sewing and beading needles

Glue stick

Double-sided tape

Scissors

Pencil

Paper cutter or craft knife and metal ruler

Craft foam (12 x 18-inch sheet)

Perforating tool

Scoring tool and bone paper folder (optional)

CLASSIC CARDS

8. Center and mount the completed work piece (page 16) onto the purple cardstock using double-sided tape. To finish, similarly mount these layers onto the front of the base card.

VARIATION

Napkins frequently sport borders of various widths and designs. Try using the entire border (or borders) of a cocktail napkin to completely frame the front of a card, as shown in the variation. Then all that's needed to finish the card is a simple center design. For the center of this African-inspired card, a tribal mask was stamped onto a square of white cardstock, colored in with watercolor pencils, then attached with double-sided tape.

Pop-up Pansies

Individual flowers are cut from the napkin then arranged like a montage in the center of this card. Tiny self-sticking foam supports beneath the flowers raise them from the surface and make them literally pop off the page.

YOU'LL NEED

PAPERS

Cardstock: white, medium green, purple, pink (8½ x 11-inch sheets)

Paper napkin with pansy design in purple, yellow, and white

Adhesive-backed paper (8½ x 11-inch sheet)

EMBELLISHMENT

Variegated gold/green/purple metallic thread #4 braid

SUPPLIES

At least 25 small double-sided adhesive foam squares or dots (or substitute foam tape cut in ¼-inch squares)

Hand-sewing needle

Double-sided tape

Scissors

Pencil

Paper cutter or craft knife and metal ruler

Craft foam (12 x 18-inch sheet)

Perforating tool

Scoring tool and bone paper folder (optional)

1. **CUT THE PAPERS:** From the white cardstock, cut a 3¼-inch square for the work piece. From the green cardstock, cut a 3¼-inch square. From the purple cardstock, cut a 4¾-inch square. From the pink cardstock, cut a rectangle 5 x 10 inches for the base card. From the napkin, cut a quadrant (or more if needed) with pansies.

2. Score and fold the pink base card (page 16) in half to form a 5-inch square.

3. Review Before You Begin at the start of this chapter.

4. **PREPARE THE NAPKIN:** Separate the napkin layers and discard all but the printed top layer. Roughly cut a circle around each of the pansies you want to use. You'll need approximately six pansies in assorted sizes and colors. Cut the sheet of adhesive-backed paper in half, reserving one half for another project. Remove the backing from the other half and place it face up on the work surface. Place the rough-cut pansies on the adhesive and gently press them into position. Smooth the napkin pansies with your fingers, rubbing gently to remove any wrinkles. Carefully cut away the background from each pansy, following the curves of the petals.

5. **COMPLETE THE WORK PIECE:** Place the pansies on the white square in a pleasing arrangement, with the larger flowers in the center and the smaller flowers tucked around them, overlapping slightly. Once you're satisfied with the arrangement, remove the paper backing from one side of the little foam pieces and place them on the back of each petal and the centers of the pansies. These will help strengthen as well as raise the pansy images. Peel the backing from the other side of the foam pieces and place the pansies in position on the work piece.

6. Center and mount the green cardstock (page 16) onto the purple cardstock using double-sided tape. Similarly center and mount the work piece on point over the sage and purple cardstocks.

7. **ADD THE EMBROIDERY:** Using the perforating tool, make a hole in the purple cardstock at every corner of the white and green cardstock. Using the variegated thread, stitch to outline the white cardstock, then stitch to outline the green cardstock. Slide the thread beneath the pansies as you stitch, if necessary.

8. To finish, center and mount all layers onto the front of the base card using double-sided tape.

African Masks

These mounted mask motifs, with their fiber headdresses, look almost like the real things. The card makes use of a variety of background papers to offset the two images, and the interesting fibers give it touchability.

YOU'LL NEED

PAPERS

Cardstock: gold pearl, bronze pearl, copper pearl, black, beige (8½ x 11-inch sheets)

Decorative paper with black/brown abstract design

Paper napkin with African mask design

Adhesive-backed paper (8½ x 11-inch sheet)

EMBELLISHMENTS

Two different bronze-colored decorative fibers (one foot of each)

Gold metallic thread

SUPPLIES

Approximately 12 small double-sided adhesive foam squares or dots (or substitute foam tape cut in ¼-inch squares)

Hand-sewing needle

Glue stick

Double-sided tape

Scissors

Pencil

Paper cutter or craft knife and metal ruler

Craft foam (12 x 18-inch sheet)

Perforating tool

Scoring tool and bone paper folder (optional)

1. **CUT THE PAPERS:** From the gold pearl cardstock, cut two rectangles 1¾ x 3½ inches each. These will be the work pieces. From the bronze pearl cardstock, cut a rectangle 2 x 6 inches. From the copper pearl cardstock, cut a rectangle 2 x 6 inches. From the black cardstock, cut a rectangle 4¼ x 6¼ inches. From the beige cardstock, cut a rectangle 6¼ x 9½ inches for the base card. From the decorative black/brown paper, cut a strip 1½ x 4¾ inches. From the napkin, cut a quadrant with at least two masks.

2. Score and fold the beige base card (page 16) in half to form a rectangle 4¾ x 6¼.

3. Review Before You Begin at the start of this chapter.

4. **PREPARE THE NAPKIN:** Separate the napkin layers and discard all but the printed top layer. Cut a rectangle 4½ x 5½ inches from the adhesive-backed paper; reserve the remainder for other projects. Remove the backing from the adhesive paper and place it adhesive side up on the work surface. Roughly cut a circle around each of the two masks you want to use. Place the rough-cut masks on the adhesive and gently press them into position. Smooth the napkin masks with your fingers, rubbing gently to remove any wrinkles. Carefully cut away the background from each mask.

5. **COMPLETE THE WORK PIECES:** Remove the paper backing from one side of the little foam pieces and place them on the back of each mask at the top, middle, and bottom. These will help strengthen as well as raise the masks. Peel the backing from the other side of the foam pieces and place one mask on each gold pearl work piece. Leave room under the tops of the masks to attach the fibers.

6. Using the perforating tool, make a hole in the gold pearl work pieces behind the top of each mask. Wrap one length of fiber around three fingers. Remove the wrapped fiber loop from your fingers and set it aside. Using the gold metallic thread and needle, come up through the hole just made. Center the fiber loop over the hole and stitch over the fiber, back into the hole, to secure it to the work piece. Cut the ends of the loop to separate the fibers. In the same manner, attach the other length of fiber to the second mask.

7. Using double-sided tape, center and mount the bronze pearl and copper pearl rectangles (page 16) side by side onto the black rectangle. Center and mount the black/brown strip onto the bronze and copper layer. Mount one completed work piece at the top of the bronze section and one at the bottom of the copper section. To finish, center and mount these layers onto the front of the base card.

TIP

When a napkin has only one or two images that are usable, as was the case with the African masks napkin, use a variety of backgrounds to create different cards. For example, cut several colors of cardstock into halves or quarters and then piece them back together, mixing up the colors, to make the cards distinctive.

Captured Hearts

A paper napkin with small squares of a repeated design is embellished with beads and stitching to create the hand-quilted look of this note card.

YOU'LL NEED

PAPERS

Cardstock: dark blue, rose (8½ x 11-inch sheets)

Paper napkin with small repeating heart-block design (or other repeating block design)

Adhesive-backed paper (8½ x 11-inch sheet)

EMBELLISHMENTS

Mauve metallic thread #4 braid

Purple metallic thread

Metallic purple seed beads (enough to outline the design in the blocks; see Tip)

SUPPLIES

Hand-sewing and beading needles

Glue stick

Double-sided tape

Scissors

Pencil

Paper cutter or craft knife and metal ruler

Craft foam (12 x 18-inch sheet)

Perforating tool

Scoring tool and bone paper folder (optional)

1. **CUT THE PAPERS:** From the dark blue cardstock, cut a rectangle 3¼ x 4½ inches for the work piece. From the rose cardstock, cut a rectangle 5 x 7 inches for the base card. From the napkin, cut a quadrant with at least six squares of a repeating design.

2. Score and fold the rose base card (page 16) in half to form a rectangle 3½ x 5 inches.

3. Review Before You Begin at the start of this chapter.

4. **PREPARE THE NAPKIN:** Separate the napkin layers and discard all but the printed top layer. Cut a rectangle 4½ x 5½ inches from the adhesive-backed paper; reserve the remainder for other projects. Remove the backing from the adhesive paper and place it adhesive side up on the work surface. Roughly cut out a section of the napkin that includes six squares with a repeating design not larger than 2¾ x 4 inches. Place the rough-cut section on the adhesive and gently press it into position. Smooth the napkin with your fingers, rubbing gently to remove any wrinkles. Carefully cut around the squares to form a rectangle. Center and glue the reinforced napkin piece onto the dark blue work piece.

5. Using the perforating tool, make a hole in the outside corners of each of the six squares. These will be used to stitch the outlines of the squares. Using the mauve metallic thread, make four long vertical stitches to outline the sides of the squares, then three long horizontal stitches to outline the squares on top and bottom.

6. **SEW ON BEADS:** Using the perforating tool, make holes around the two middle hearts, spacing them evenly and far enough apart to fit each bead. The size and type of the repeating motif used will determine how many beads you will need to sew on each. Following the instructions for adding beads (page 15), and using the purple metallic thread and beading needle, sew the metallic purple beads in place around the hearts at each hole.

7. To finish, center and mount the completed work piece (page 16) onto the front of the base card using double-sided tape.

TIP
Any napkin with squares of a repeating motif can be used to make
this card. Cut the adhesive-backed paper slightly larger all around
than the number of design squares used. The seed beads can be used
to outline the motif in the center squares, in alternating squares, or
in the corner squares.

Simple Quilt Block

A paper napkin with a collage design allows you to select from among a number of interesting images and combine them with embroidery to make this simple quilt-block card.

YOU'LL NEED

PAPERS

Cardstock: dark brown, light brown (8½ x 11-inch sheets)

Green/brown mottled decorative paper (8½ x 11-inch sheet)

Paper napkin with a collage design in browns

Adhesive-backed paper (8½ x 11-inch sheet)

EMBELLISHMENT

Variegated gold/copper/black metallic thread

SUPPLIES

Hand-sewing needle

Glue stick

Removable tape

Double-sided tape

Scissors

Pencil

Template with squares of different sizes

Paper cutter or craft knife and metal ruler

Craft foam (12 x 18-inch sheet)

Perforating tool

Scoring tool and bone paper folder (optional)

1. **CUT THE PAPERS:** From the dark brown cardstock, cut a 4¾-inch square for the work piece. From the light brown cardstock, cut a rectangle 5¼ x 10½ inches for the base card. From the green/brown paper, cut a 5-inch square. From the napkin, cut a quadrant.

2. Score and fold the light brown base card (page 16) in half to form a 5¼-inch square.

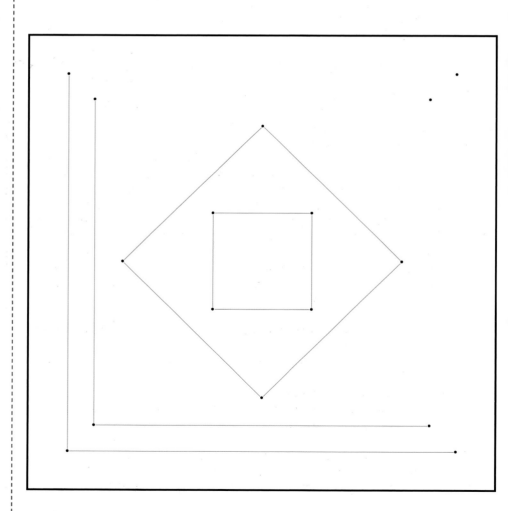

3. Following the instructions in Getting Started (page 13), transfer the embroidery pattern to the dark brown work piece, making the necessary perforations.

4. Review Before You Begin at the start of this chapter.

5. **EMBROIDER THE PATTERN:** With the pattern markings to guide you, and using the variegated metallic thread, outline the center square from corner to corner. Carry the thread to the diamond and outline it in the same manner. Repeat with the two outer-most squares. The stitching will act as a guide for placing the napkin pieces.

6. **PREPARE THE NAPKIN:** Separate the napkin layers and discard all but the printed top layer. Cut the sheet of adhesive-backed paper in half, reserving one half for another project. Using the template or ruler, draw five 1-inch squares on the front of the adhesive paper; cut them out. Select five images on the napkin you want to use. Pick the most interesting one for the center square; the others will be cut to make the triangle pieces. One at a time, remove the backing from the cut adhesive squares and place them on the back of the napkin over the chosen images; gently press them into position. Smooth the napkin with your fingers, rubbing gently to remove any wrinkles. Cut out the reinforced napkin squares. Cut four squares in half on the diagonal to make eight triangles.

7. Using the stitched pattern and photograph as guides, position the small square inside the stitched border of the center square, trimming the sides if it is too large. Glue the square in place. Glue one triangle in each of the four corners of the stitched diamond. Try to have the sides touching to make a nice frame around the center square. Glue the remaining triangles in the four corners of the smaller of the two outer squares.

8. Center and mount the completed work piece (page 16) onto the green/brown decorative paper square using double-sided tape. To finish, similarly mount these layers onto the front of the base card.

Basket-Weave Quilt Block

The autumn colors of the napkin set the theme for this card, which is embellished with an embroidered basket block that reminds us it's harvest time. A great card for writing a thank-you note to your Thanksgiving hosts.

YOU'LL NEED

PAPERS

Cardstock: burgundy, gold, ivory
(8½ x 11-inch sheets)

Paper napkin with leaf design in
autumn colors

Adhesive-backed paper
(8½ x 11-inch sheet)

EMBELLISHMENT

Gold metallic thread

SUPPLIES

Hand-sewing needle

Glue stick

Removable tape

Double-sided tape

Scissors

Pencil

Template with squares of different
sizes

Paper cutter or craft knife and
metal ruler

Craft foam (12 x 18-inch sheet)

Perforating tool

Scoring tool and bone paper
folder (optional)

1. **CUT THE PAPERS:** From the burgundy cardstock, cut a 4¾-inch square for the work piece. From the gold cardstock, cut a 5-inch square. From the ivory cardstock, cut a 5¼ x 10½-inch square for the base card. From the napkin, cut a quadrant.

2. Score and fold the ivory base card (page 16) in half to form a 5¼-inch square.

3. Following the instructions in Getting Started (page 13), transfer the embroidery pattern to the burgundy work piece, making the necessary perforations.

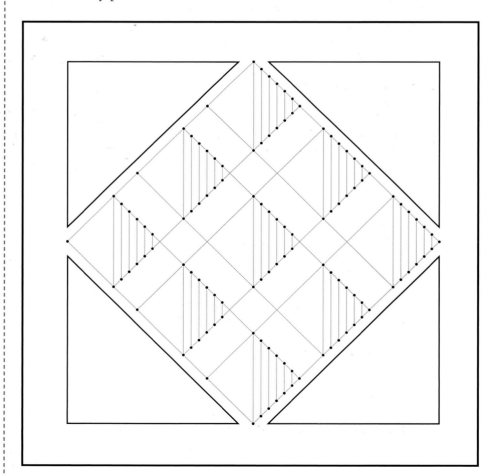

4. Review Before You Begin at the start of this chapter.

5. **EMBROIDER THE PATTERN:** With the pattern markings to guide you, and using the gold metallic thread, stitch the triangles that will be half of the nine small squares that comprise the center design of the card. Begin at the center of the top square and make six vertical stitches, from long to short, to create the first triangle. Move from square to square, stitching the triangle portion of each in the same manner. Carry the thread to a corner hole on the outside of the large center square and make six long stitches to outline the top and bottom of the rows of squares. Similarly make another six long stitches to outline the sides of the rows of squares. The stitched pattern will act as a guide for placing the napkin pieces.

6. **PREPARE THE NAPKIN:** Separate the napkin layers and discard all but the printed top layer. Cut the sheet of adhesive-backed paper in half, reserving one half for another project. Using the template or ruler, draw five ¾-inch squares and two 1¾-inch squares on the front of the adhesive paper; cut them out. Select the portions of the napkin you want to use. One at a time, remove the backing from the cut adhesive squares and place them on the back of the napkin over the chosen images; gently press them into position. Smooth the napkin with your fingers, rubbing gently to remove any wrinkles. Cut out the reinforced napkin squares. Cut each square in half on the diagonal to make ten small and four large triangles.

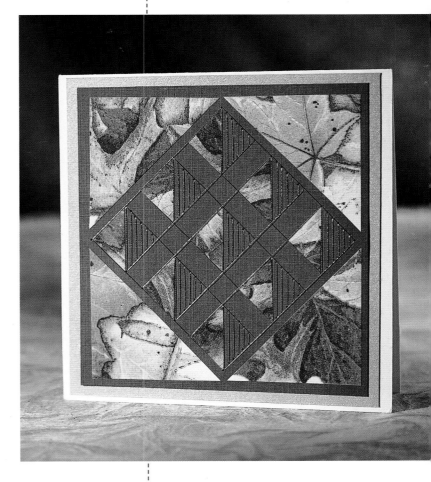

7. Using the stitched pattern and photograph as guides, glue a small napkin triangle beside each stitched triangle to complete the nine small squares in the center square. Trim the napkin triangles if necessary, so the napkin does not extend beyond the stitching. Glue one large napkin triangle about ¹⁄₁₆ inch from each outlined side of the large center square, making sure the base of each triangle is even with the corners of the large square.

8. Center and mount the completed work piece (page 16) onto the gold cardstock using double-sided tape. To finish, similarly mount these layers onto the front of the base card.

Blue-on-Black Quilt Block

Some napkin designs are so beautiful they practically beg to be a made into a card. Here the blues and gold of the formal print harmonize elegantly with the gold-on-black embroidery to produce a sophisticated and dramatic card.

YOU'LL NEED

PAPERS

Cardstock: black, robin's-egg blue, white (8½ x 11-inch sheets)

Paper napkin with a design in royal blue/gold/purple

Adhesive-backed paper (8½ x 11-inch sheet

EMBELLISHMENT

Antique-gold thread #4 braid

SUPPLIES

Hand-sewing needle

Glue stick

Removable tape

Double-sided tape

Scissors

Pencil

Template with squares of different sizes

Paper cutter or craft knife and metal ruler

Craft foam (12 x 18-inch sheet)

Perforating tool

Scoring tool and bone paper folder (optional)

1. **CUT THE PAPERS:** From the black cardstock, cut a 5-inch square for the work piece. From the robin's-egg blue cardstock, cut a 5¼-inch square. From the white cardstock, cut a rectangle 5½ x 11 inches for the base card. From the napkin, cut a quadrant.

2. Score and fold the white base card (page 16) in half to form a 5½-inch square.

3. Following the instructions in Getting Started (page 13), transfer the embroidery pattern to the black work piece, making the necessary perforations.

4. Review Before You Begin at the start of this chapter.

5. **EMBROIDER THE PATTERN:** With the pattern markings to guide you, and using the antique-gold thread, stitch the eight small triangles near the corners of the card. Each triangle is comprised of three graduated parallel stitches. Next, stitch the four small squares in the larger center square. Stitch the two innermost sides on each first, then stitch the large square from corner to corner to outline

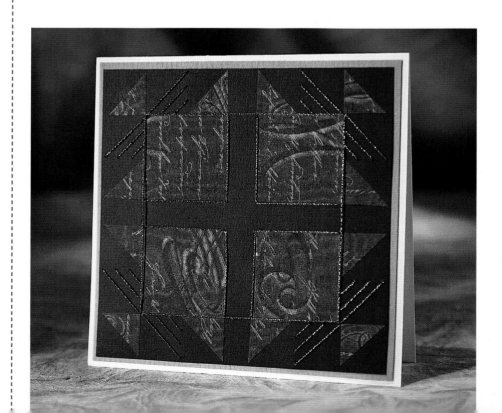

both the large and small squares. The stitching will act as a guide for placing the napkin pieces.

6. **PREPARE THE NAPKIN:** Separate the napkin layers and discard all but the printed top layer. Cut the sheet of adhesive-backed paper in half, reserving one half for another project. Using the template or ruler, draw six ¾-inch squares and four 1½-inch squares on the front of the adhesive paper; cut them out. Select the portions of the napkin you want to use. One at a time, remove the backing from the cut adhesive squares and place them on the back of the napkin over the chosen images; gently press them into position. Smooth the napkin with your fingers, rubbing gently to remove any wrinkles. Cut out the reinforced napkin squares. Cut the small squares in half on the diagonal to make twelve triangles.

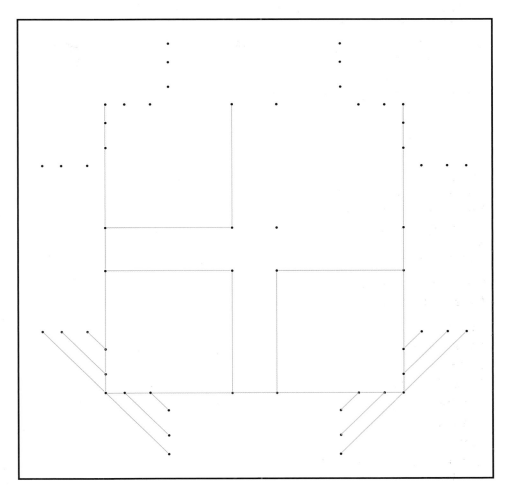

7. Using the stitched pattern and photograph as guides, glue the napkin squares inside the stitched center squares. Trim the napkin squares if necessary, so they don't extend beyond the stitching. Glue four napkin triangles so that each right angle abuts a corner of the large stitched square and is centered between the two stitched triangles. Glue the remaining eight triangles outside the stitched large square so that their right angles align with the outer corners of each stitched napkin square.

8. Center and mount the completed work piece (page 16) onto the robin's-egg blue cardstock using double-sided tape. To finish, similarly mount these layers onto the front of the base card.

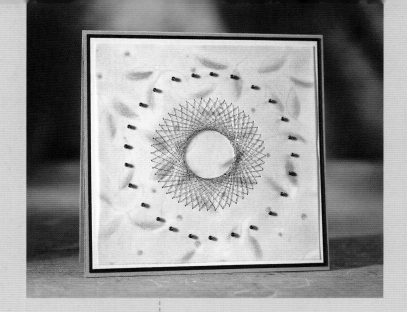

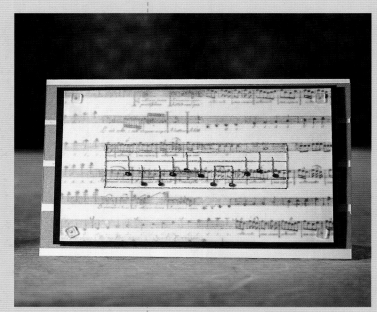

6

Embroidery and Beads on Vellum

BEFORE YOU BEGIN

You've already seen how using embroidery and beads on plain cardstock can result in beautifully decorated cards. In this chapter vellum is added to the mix. Vellum is a crisp, semitransparent paper with a very smooth, satin finish. Because it is available in so many patterns and colors, it makes a wonderful background for the embellishments. Placed over cardstock of any color, vellums impart a soft, muted look and a subtle underpattern to the embroidery.

Before embroidering on vellum, it must be attached to a piece of cardstock to stabilize it and give it needed support. Often white or ivory cardstock is used as a backing because many vellums brighten up when placed on these colors. When choosing a white-based vellum, try putting different colors of cardstock behind it to see on which one the pattern or print shows more clearly.

Vellum can be attached to cardstock in several ways. An acid-free glue that can be brushed on in a thin layer will work well for most vellums. Also available is a vellum tape that is specially made to be invisible when used; however, using a small piece of clean, double-sided transparent tape in the corners can also work well on most opaque vellums. Another way to affix the vellum to the cardstock is with brads or scrapbook nails. These items add a decorative touch of their own, so if you decide to use them, select ones that complement the vellum or the overall look of the card.

Once the vellum is attached to the cardstock, the unit becomes the work piece, and you can transfer the patterns provided. After the holes are perforated, embroider the design as instructed. Always add beads last.

Mauve Filigree

This delicate embroidery design recalls the intricate ornamental openwork of Victorian gold and silver jewelry. The same pattern can be used to create a simple contemporary floral design.

YOU'LL NEED

PAPERS

Cardstock: mauve pearl, black, white, ivory (8½ x 11-inch sheets)

White vellum with decorative writing

Metallic mauve decorative paper (8½ x 11-inch sheet)

EMBELLISHMENTS

Purple metallic thread

Metallic purple seed beads (8)

SUPPLIES

Hand-sewing and beading needles

Removable tape

Double-sided tape

Acid-free brush-on craft glue or rubber cement (optional)

Scissors

Pencil

Paper cutter or craft knife and metal ruler

Craft foam (12 x 18-inch sheet)

Perforating tool

Scoring tool and bone paper folder (optional)

1. **CUT THE PAPERS:** From the mauve pearl cardstock, cut a 2¾-inch square for the work piece. From the black cardstock, cut a 3-inch square. From the white cardstock, cut a 4¾-inch square. From the ivory cardstock, cut a rectangle 5¼ x 10½ inches for the base card. From the vellum, cut a 4¾-inch square. From the metallic mauve paper, cut a 5-inch square.

2. Score and fold the ivory base card (page 16) in half to form a 5¼-inch square.

4. Following the instructions in Getting Started (page 13), transfer the embroidery pattern to the work piece, making the necessary perforations.

5. Review Before You Begin at the start of this chapter.

6. **EMBROIDER THE PATTERN:** With the pattern markings to guide you, and using the purple metallic thread, stitch the four small center squares. Stitch the four-point design first, then stitching diagonally from corner to corner of each square, make the X on top of the four-point design. Using long stitches from corner to corner, stitch the square outlining the four center blocks. Stitch the lines dividing the four center blocks. Stitch the outermost square.

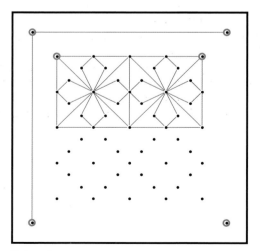

⊙ **bead**

7. **SEW ON BEADS:** Following the instructions for adding beads (page 15), and using the purple metallic thread and beading needle, sew the metallic purple beads in place at each corner of the center block and the outermost square.

8. Center and mount the completed work piece (page 16) onto the black square using double-sided tape. Using either glue or double-sided tape in the corners only, align and mount the vellum onto the white square. Center and mount the layered work piece onto the vellum using double-sided tape. Similarly mount these layers onto the metallic mauve square. To finish, center and mount all layers onto the front of the base card using double-sided tape.

VARIATION

This same embroidery pattern can be stitched to create a different design, as shown. Cut a 3½-inch square from both the white cardstock and flowered vellum. Mount the vellum onto the white square to form the work piece. Transfer the pattern. Use the pattern markings of the small stitching diagram and green metallic thread to stitch the stylized floral squares that form the center square, then stitch the outer square. Add eight green beads as shown. Center and mount the completed work piece onto a 3¾-inch square cut from sage green cardstock. Then mount these layers onto a 4 × 8-inch rectangle cut from pink cardstock and folded in half to form the base card.

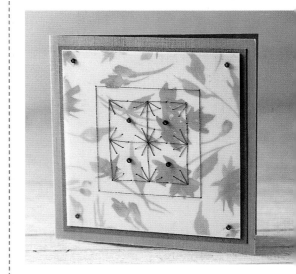

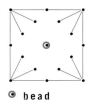

ⓒ **bead**

Sheet Music

On this three-dimensional card the vellum's music motif is repeated in the embroidered and beaded design. To hold the mounted layers together, tiny scrapbook nails are used in the corners.

YOU'LL NEED

PAPERS

Cardstock: white, black, and gold pearl (8½ x 11-inch sheets: 2 sheets white, 1 each black and gold)

Vellum printed with music notation design

EMBELLISHMENTS

Gold metallic thread #4 braid

Bronze seed beads (11)

SUPPLIES

Hand-sewing and beading needles

4 clear scrapbook nails

At least 15 small double-sided adhesive foam squares or dots (or substitute foam tape cut in ¼-inch squares)

Removable tape

Double-sided tape

Scissors

Pencil

Paper cutter or craft knife and metal ruler

Craft foam (12 x 18-inch sheet)

Perforating tool

Scoring tool and bone paper folder (optional)

1. **CUT THE PAPERS:** From the white cardstock, cut a rectangle 3½ x 6 inches for the work piece and one 6¾ x 8 inches for the base card. From the black cardstock, cut a rectangle 3¾ x 6¼ inches. From the gold pearl cardstock, cut four strips ¾ x 6¾ inches. From the vellum, cut a rectangle 3½ x 6 inches.

2. Score and fold the white base card (page 16) in half to form a 4 x 6¾-inch rectangle.

3. Using removable tape at the edges, align and secure the vellum onto the small white rectangle. This is now the work piece.

4. Following the instructions in Getting Started (page 13), transfer the embroidery pattern to the work piece, making the necessary perforations.

5. Review Before You Begin at the start of this chapter.

6. **EMBROIDER THE PATTERN:** With the pattern markings to guide you, and using the gold metallic thread, stitch all of the music notes. Stitch the horizontal lines of the staff over the notes already stitched.

7. **SEW ON BEADS:** Following the instructions for adding beads (page 15), and using the gold metallic thread and beading needle, sew a bronze seed bead onto the end of each stitched note. Remove the tape holding the vellum and cardstock together.

8. Center the completed work piece (page 16) onto the black rectangle. Following the manufacturer's instructions, insert a scrapbook nail into each corner of the work piece and through the black rectangle to hold the layers together.

9. Using double-sided tape, affix the four gold strips to the front of the base card, spacing them equidistantly.

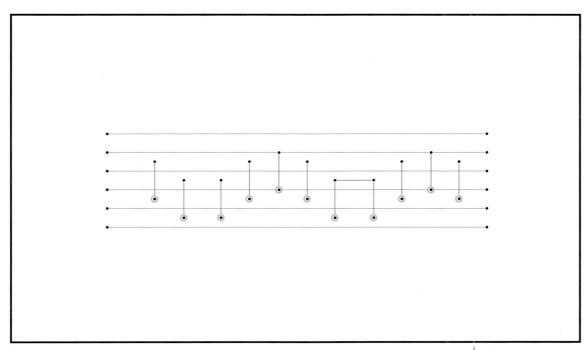

⊙ **bead**

10. Remove the paper backing from one side of the little foam pieces and place them on the back of the black rectangle at the top, middle, sides, and bottom. This will raise the work piece to allow room for the backs of the scrapbook nails. Peel the backing from the other side of the foam pieces and adhere the mounted work piece, centered, to the front of the base card.

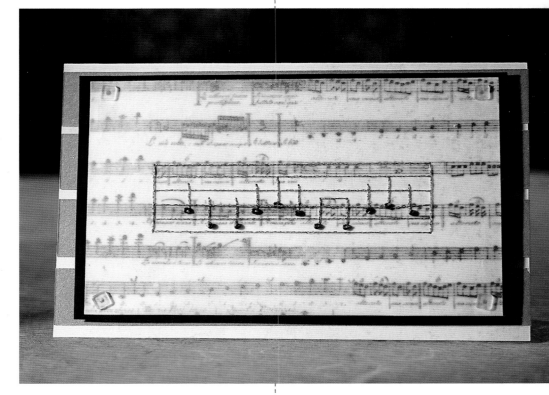

Circle of Moonbeams

Silver bugle beads radiate like moonbeams from the stitches of this simple circular design. On this card the embroidery, rather than glue or tape, secures the vellum to the cardstock.

YOU'LL NEED

PAPERS

Cardstock: white, rust, ivory
 (8½ x 11-inch sheets)

Soft peach vellum with printed words

Metallic gold/silver mottled paper (8½ x 11-inch sheet)

EMBELLISHMENTS

Gold metallic thread

Silver bugle beads (20)

SUPPLIES

Hand-sewing and beading needles

Removable tape

Double-sided tape

Scissors

Pencil

Paper cutter or craft knife and metal ruler

Craft foam (12 x 18-inch sheet)

Perforating tool

Scoring tool and bone paper folder (optional)

1. **CUT THE PAPERS:** From the white cardstock, cut a 4½-inch square for the work piece. From the rust cardstock, cut a 5¼-inch square. From the ivory cardstock, cut a rectangle 5½ x 11 inches.

2. Score and fold the ivory base card (page 16) in half to form a 5½-inch square.

3. Using removable tape at the edges, align and secure the vellum onto the white square. This is now the work piece.

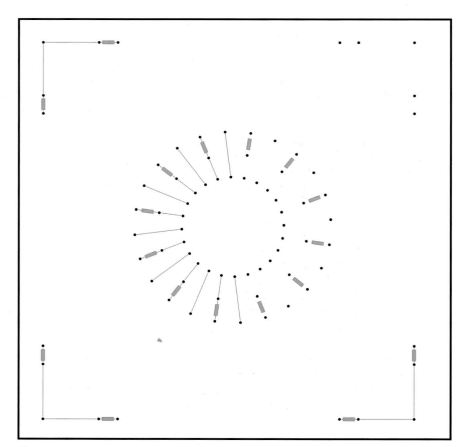

▌ bead

4. Following the instructions in Getting Started (page 13), transfer the embroidery pattern to the work piece, making the necessary perforations.

5. Review Before You Begin at the start of this chapter.

6. **EMBROIDER THE PATTERN:** With the pattern markings to guide you, and using the gold metallic thread, make long straight stitches from the innermost circle to the outermost. Then make smaller stitches from the inner circle to the middle circle. Continue to alternate between these large and small stitches, working around the circle. Outline each corner with two right-angled stitches, from the corner out to each side.

7. **SEW ON BEADS:** Following the instructions for adding beads (page 15), and using the gold metallic thread and beading needle, sew a bugle bead at the end of each stitch in the four corners of the card. Sew a bugle bead at the end of every short stitch in the circle design: Come up with the beading needle at the free hole on the outmost circle, slide on a bead, and go into the hole of the small stitch in the center circle. Continue in this manner to sew on all beads at the circumference of the circle. Remove the tape holding the vellum and cardstock together.

8. Center and mount the completed work piece (page 16) to the metallic gold/silver paper using double-sided tape. Similarly, center and mount these layers onto the rust square. To finish, mount all layers onto the front of the base card.

Framed Beaded Cross-stitch

The beautiful, detailed stitching on vellum dappled like a Monet watercolor, is framed to highlight the beadwork and embroidery. With its springtime colors, this card is a perfect choice for Mother's Day.

YOU'LL NEED

PAPERS

Cardstock: white, lime green, gold pearl (8½ x 11-inch sheets)

Vellum with an all-over pastel floral design

EMBELLISHMENTS

Lime green metallic thread #4 braid

Green metallic thread

Green seed beads (25)

SUPPLIES

Template for 2½-inch square and cutting tool

Hand-sewing and beading needles

Removable tape

Double-sided tape

Acid-free brush-on craft glue or rubber cement (optional)

Scissors

Pencil

Paper cutter or craft knife and metal ruler

Craft foam (12 x 18-inch sheet)

Perforating tool

Scoring tool and bone paper folder (optional)

1. **CUT THE PAPERS:** From the white cardstock, cut a rectangle 4½ x 5¼ inches for the work piece and a rectangle 5¾ x 10 inches for the base card. From the lime green cardstock, cut a rectangle 4 x 5 inches. From the gold pearl cardstock, cut a rectangle 4¾ x 5½ inches. From the vellum, cut a rectangle 4½ x 5¼ inches.

2. Score and fold the white base card (page 16) in half to form a 5 x 5¾-inch rectangle.

3. **PREPARE THE WORK PIECE:** Using either brush-on glue or double-sided tape in the corners only, center and mount the vellum onto the small white rectangle. This is now the work piece.

4. Center the embroidery pattern on the work piece and, following the instructions in Getting Started (page 13), transfer the pattern, making the necessary perforations.

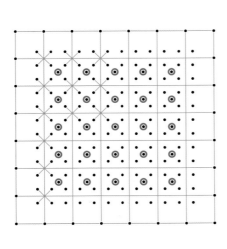

⊙ **bead**

5. Review Before You Begin at the start of this chapter.

6. **EMBROIDER THE PATTERN:** With the pattern markings to guide you, and using the lime green metallic thread, stitch the vertical lines of the pattern. Next, stitch all the horizontal lines. Stitch an X over each point where the horizontal and vertical lines meet. Make sure the bottom stitches of the Xs are going in the same direction and the cross-stitches are all going in the opposite direction.

7. **SEW ON BEADS:** Following the instructions for adding beads (page 15), and using the green metallic thread and beading needle, sew the green seed beads in place in the center of each small square that has been formed by the stitching.

8. **MAKE THE FRAME:** Using the template and cutting tool, cut out a 2½-inch square frame in the center of the wrong side of the lime green rectangle. Turn the frame right side up and center and mount it over the completed embroidery using double-sided tape.

9. Center and mount the framed vellum work piece (page 16) onto the gold pearl rectangle. To finish, similarly mount these layers onto the front of the base card.

TIP
Placing a frame over the vellum is a way to hide the adhesive used. When attaching the vellum, make sure to apply the glue or tape under the areas the frame will cover.

Daisy Love

For this card, a colored cardstock used behind the vellum allowed the printed words to be clearly seen, and in doing so, the message became the inspiration for the embroidered design.

YOU'LL NEED

PAPERS

Cardstock: medium blue, lime green, white (8½ x 11-inch sheets)

Vellum with "loves me, loves me not" printed on it, or vellum of choice

EMBELLISHMENTS

Gold metallic thread

Blue metallic thread

Metallic blue seed beads (8)

SUPPLIES

Hand-sewing and beading needles

Acid-free brush-on craft glue or rubber cement (optional)

Removable tape

Double-sided tape

Scissors

Pencil

Paper cutter or craft knife and metal ruler

Craft foam (12 x 18-inch sheet)

Perforating tool

Scoring tool and bone paper folder (optional)

1. **CUT THE PAPERS:** From the medium blue cardstock, cut a 4¼-inch square for the work piece and a 5-inch square. From the lime green cardstock, cut a 4¾-inch square. From the white cardstock, cut a rectangle 5¼ x 10½ inches for the base card. From the vellum, cut a 4¼-inch square.

2. Score and fold the white base card (page 16) in half to form a 5¼-inch square.

⊙ **bead**

3. Using either brush-on glue or double-sided tape in the corners only, align and mount the vellum onto the smaller blue square. This is now the work piece.

4. Following the instructions in Getting Started (page 13), transfer the embroidery pattern to the work piece, making the necessary perforations.

5. Review Before You Begin at the start of this chapter.

6. **EMBROIDER THE PATTERN:** With the pattern markings to guide you, and using the gold metallic thread, stitch the daisy. Begin with the sides of the petals, which are comprised of three graduated stitches. Come out at hole A and go into hole 1, return to A and go into hole 11. Return to A, go into B. Return to A, go into C. Repeat to stitch all petals. Next, stitch the tips of the petals. Come up hole 1 and go into hole 5. Continue stitching in the following sequence: 6 – 2, 3 – 7, 8 – 4, 5 – 9, 10 – 6, 7 – 11.

7. Using the blue metallic thread, stitch from hole A to holes 1 and 11 to outline the longest of the gold stitches at the sides of each petal. Make smaller stitches from A into hole C between each petal.

8. **SEW ON BEADS:** Following the instructions for adding beads (page 15), and using the blue metallic thread and beading needle, sew the blue seed beads in place at hole C between each petal.

9. Center and mount the work piece (page 16) onto the lime green square using double-sided tape. Similarly center and mount these layers onto the medium blue square. To finish, center and mount all layers onto the front of the base card.

Sunburst

The soft green-leaf print of the vellum peeks from under the iridescent blending filament used to form the circular center motif, around which the beads gather like planets around the sun.

YOU'LL NEED

PAPERS

Cardstock: white, dark green, and medium green (8½ x 11-inch sheets)

Vellum with green-leaf pattern (8½ x 11-inch sheet)

EMBELLISHMENTS

Variegated gold/green metallic blending filament

Metallic green seed beads (25)

SUPPLIES

Hand-sewing and beading needles

Removable tape

Double-sided tap

Acid-free brush-on craft glue or rubber cement (optional)

Scissors

Pencil

Paper cutter or craft knife and metal ruler

Craft foam (12 x 18-inch sheet)

Perforating tool

Scoring tool and bone paper folder (optional)

1. **CUT THE PAPERS:** From the white cardstock, cut a 5-inch square for the work piece. From the dark green cardstock, cut a 5¼-inch square. From the medium green cardstock, cut a rectangle 5½ x 11 inches for the base card. From the vellum, cut a 4¾-inch square.

2. Score and fold the medium green base card (page 16) in half to form a 5½-inch square.

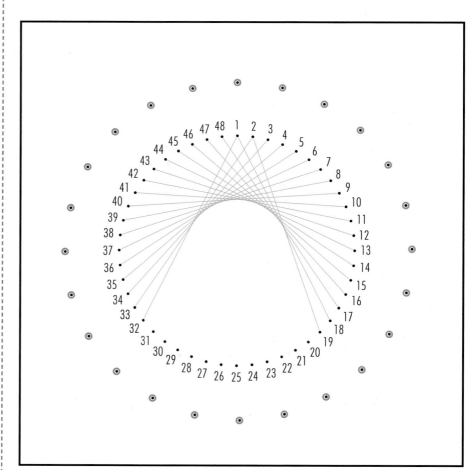

⊙ **bead**

3. **PREPARE THE WORK PIECE:** Using either brush-on glue or double-sided tape in the corners only, center and mount the vellum onto the white square. This is now the work piece.

4. Following the instructions in Getting Started (page 00), transfer the embroidery pattern to the work piece, making the necessary perforations.

5. Review Before You Begin at the start of this chapter.

6. **EMBROIDER THE PATTERN:** With the pattern markings to guide you, and using the variegated blending filament, stitch the sunburst design in the center. Come out at hole 1 and go into hole 32. Continue stitching clockwise in the following sequence: 33 – 2, 3 – 34, 35 – 4, 5 – 36, 37 – 6, 7 – 38, 39 – 8, 9 – 40, 41 – 10, 11 – 42, 43 – 12, 13 – 44, 45 – 14, 15 – 46, 47 – 16, 17 – 48, 1 – 18, 19 – 2, 3 – 20, 21 – 4, 5 – 22, 23 – 6, 7 – 24, 25 – 8, 9 – 26, 27 – 10, 11 – 28, 29 – 12, 13 – 30, 31 – 14, 15 – 32, 33 – 16, 17 – 34, 35 – 18, 19 – 36, 37 – 20, 21 – 38, 39 – 22, 23 – 40, 41 – 24, 25 – 42, 43 – 26, 27 – 44, 45 – 28, 29 – 46, 47 – 30, 31 – 48.

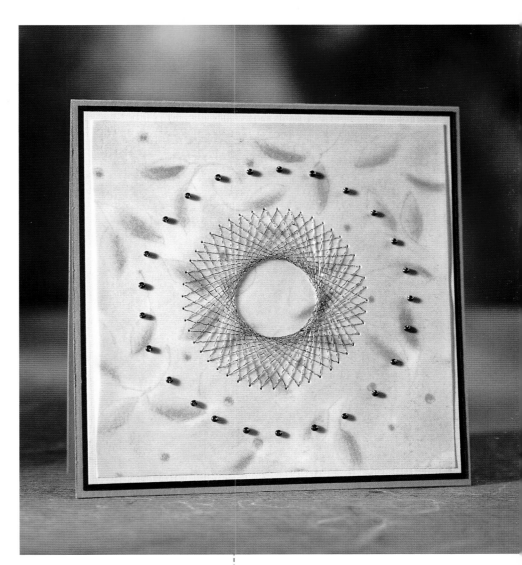

7. **SEW ON BEADS:** Following the instructions for adding beads (page 15), and using the blending filament and beading needle, sew the metallic green beads in place at each hole on the outer circle.

8. Center and mount the completed work piece (page 16) onto the dark green square using double-sided tape. To finish, similarly mount these layers onto the front of the base card.

TIP
Using vellum with a soft-colored pattern works well with this design because it doesn't detract from the intricate-looking embroidery. Select vellum colors and designs that don't overwhelm the decorative work on the card.

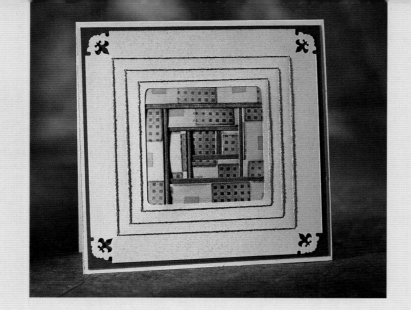

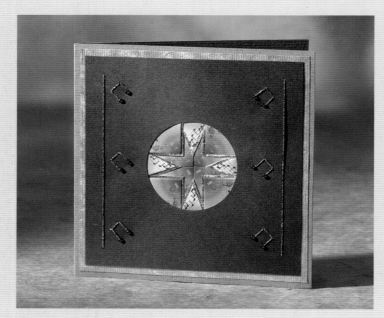

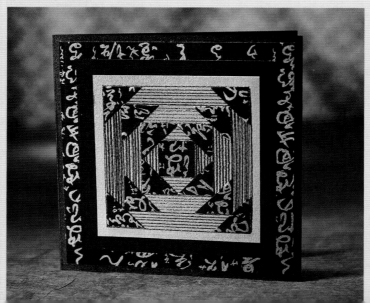

Kaleidoscope Folding

BEFORE YOU BEGIN

For centuries, children and adults have been fascinated by kaleidoscopes, with their complex, colorful designs and repeating, symmetrical patterns. Kaleidoscope cards attempt to capture this idea of repeating patterns and colors by means of a simple layering technique using paper folded into strips, squares, and kite shapes.

Similar to iris and teabag folding, this technique, which also originated in The Netherlands, uses decorative lightweight papers, such as teabag, gift wrap, and origami papers in the folding process. These lightweight papers are easy to fold and lay flat on the card, resulting in a crisp, neat appearance.

The use of paper strips in the first two projects is similar to iris folding, where the folded edges of the strips are central to the creation of the designs. The remaining projects make use of small decorative paper squares, as in teabag folding. These squares are cut in half diagonally, and, using similar origami folds, are folded into either squares or kite shapes, which are then layered sequentially and by color to produce the kaleidoscope design. This layering also results in designs with intriguing three-dimensional effects and a sense of depth.

The layering sequence for each card is explained in detail with every project. As with many other cards in this book, decorative embroidery is often integrated into the overall design and, in one card, even substitutes for layered paper strips. A template with squares or circles of varying sizes will be useful when drawing and/or cutting the appropriate shapes onto cardstock to make a frame for the finished design.

Although the kaleidoscope cards may look quite intricate, they are not at all difficult to construct. The illustrations will guide you in the placement of the folded paper strips, squares, and kites. Don't worry if you can't find the papers chosen for these projects. Trust your own creative instincts. Choose from among the many patterned and colored papers that are available to create your own distinctive kaleidoscope cards.

Log Cabin

Constructed of just two layers, this is the most basic of the kaleidoscope designs. The pattern formed by the overlapping double strips is identical to the quilt block known as the Log Cabin.

YOU'LL NEED

PAPERS

Cardstock: lime green, medium green, ivory (8½ x 11-inch sheets)

Metallic lime green paper (8½ x 11-inch sheet)

Decorative lime green patterned paper (8½ x 11-inch sheet)

EMBELLISHMENT

Lime green metallic thread #4 braid

SUPPLIES

Template for 2½-inch square and cutting tool

Decorative corner and motif punches

Hand-sewing needle

Glue stick

Tape: removable, transparent, double-sided

Scissors

Pencil

Paper cutter or craft knife and metal ruler

Craft foam (12 x 18-inch sheet)

Perforating tool

Scoring tool and bone paper folder (optional)

1. **CUT THE PAPERS:** From the lime green cardstock, cut a 3½-inch square for the kaleidoscope work piece and a 5-inch square for the embroidery. From the medium green cardstock, cut a 5¼-inch square. From the ivory cardstock, cut a rectangle 5½ x 11 inches for the base card. From the metallic and patterned papers, cut at least four ¾ x 8½-inch strips each. From the patterned paper also cut a ¾-inch square.

2. Score and fold the ivory base card (page 16) in half to form a 5½-inch square.

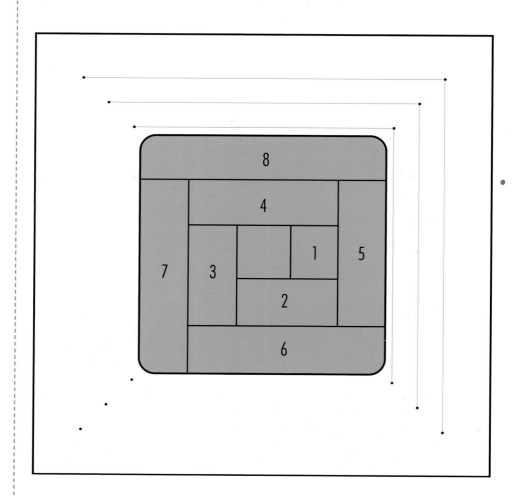

3. **MAKE THE FRAME:** Using the template and cutting tool, cut out a 2½-inch square from the center of the large lime green square to make the frame. Use the punches to decorate the corners.

4. **PREPARE THE STRIPS:** Fold each of the patterned and metallic strips of paper in half lengthwise, creating a folded edge running the width of the strip. Glue one patterned strip onto each metallic strip, folded edges in the same direction, leaving ⅛ inch of the metallic paper showing (see photograph). Run the bone paper folder, your fingernail, or the edge of a ruler along the folded edge of the double paper strips to flatten them as much as possible.

5. **CONSTRUCT THE KALEIDOSCOPE:** Using a ruler and pencil, draw two diagonal lines from corner to corner on the work piece. Where the two lines intersect is the center. Glue the small square of patterned paper onto the center of the work piece. Using either a template or ruler and pencil, draw a 2½-inch square around the patterned square. Use this drawn square as a guide to make sure the strips of paper are placed parallel to its sides.

6. Place one of the double strips along the right edge of the patterned square and cut it slightly longer than the width of the square. Glue the strip in place with the folded edge overlapping the patterned square slightly (see section 1 on the pattern). As you layer the strips to form the kaleidoscope design, cut pieces as needed from one strip until it's too short to use, then begin cutting another strip.

7. Moving clockwise, place the remainder of the first strip against the bottom edge of the patterned square and cut it long enough to cover both the bottom edge of the square and the width of the previous strip. Glue it in place with the folded edge overlapping both the patterned square and the previously glued strip (see section 2). Next, place a strip on the left edge of the patterned square and cut

it long enough to cover the side of the square and the width of the previous strip (see section 3). Glue as before. To complete the first layer of the kaleidoscope design, place a strip along the top edge of the patterned square and cut it long enough to cover the top of the square, the width of the previous strip, and the width of the first strip placed (see section 4). Glue as before.

8. To add the second layer of the design, begin at the right edge of the square again and, moving clockwise, place the strips in the same manner as the first layer, making sure the new strips slightly overlap the strips of the previous layer. Use the square drawn on the work piece as a guide for placing the strips on straight. The second layer of strips should completely cover the outline of the square drawn on the work piece. Place the cutout frame over the work piece to make sure the ends of all the papers are covered; do not attach it yet.

9. **TRANSFER AND EMBROIDER THE PATTERN:** Following the instructions in Getting Started (page 13), transfer the embroidery pattern to the cutout frame, making the necessary perforations. Using the lime green metallic thread, stitch three graduated squares around the opening of the frame. Complete the same side of the squares before moving on to the next side, stitching from left to right on the outer square, right to left on the middle square, and left to right on the inner square.

10. Tape the work piece to the back of the frame using transparent tape, making sure to center the kaleidoscope pattern so that the edges of the strips don't show through the frame.

11. Center and mount the completed framed work piece (page 16) onto the medium green cardstock using double-sided tape. To finish, similarly center and mount these layers onto the front of the base card.

VARIATION

You can change the look of this kaleidoscope pattern by using strips of two complementary papers. To make the card shown here, a solid and a patterned paper were used to form the three layers of the design. To create the first layer, the folded patterned strips were placed first: the first strip slightly overlapping the right side of the center square; the second, on the bottom. The solid strips were placed last: the third on the left side of the square; and the fourth on the top. Follow the same sequence for the next two layers to complete the pattern.

Corner Square

Folded teabag papers are used to make the corner squares of this four-layer kaleidoscope. The colorful printed paper squares are a decorative counterpoint to the solid-colored strips.

1. **CUT THE PAPERS:** From the dark blue cardstock, cut a 4¾-inch square. From the ivory cardstock, cut a 3½-inch square for the work piece and a rectangle 5¼ x 10½ inches. From the metallic lavender and ivory pearl papers, cut four ¾ x 8½-inch strips each.

2. Score and fold the ivory base card (page 16) in half to form a 5¼-inch square.

3. **MAKE THE FRAME:** Using the template and cutting tool, cut out a 3-inch square from the center of the dark blue square to make the frame.

YOU'LL NEED

PAPERS

Cardstock: dark blue, ivory (8½ x 11-inch sheets)

Metallic lavender and ivory pearl papers (8½ x 11-inch sheets)

Teabag folding paper (five 1½-inch squares) or squares cut from patterned paper

SUPPLIES

Template for 3-inch square and cutting tool

Glue stick

Transparent tape

Double-sided tape

Scissors

Pencil

Decorative edging scissors

Paper cutter or craft knife and metal ruler

Craft foam (12 x 18-inch sheet)

Scoring tool and bone paper folder (optional)

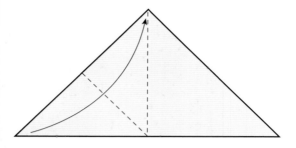

FIGURE 1

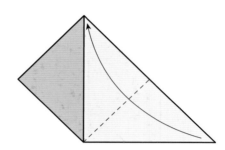

FIGURE 2

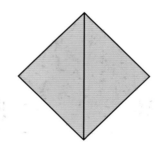

FIGURE 3

Teabag Square	13				Teabag Square
	9				
	Teabag Square	5	Teabag Square		
		1			
16	12	8	4	Teabag Square	2	6	10	14
	Teabag Square	3	Teabag Square		
		7			
Teabag Square	11				Teabag Square
	15				

4. **PREPARE THE STRIPS AND SQUARES:** Fold each strip of paper in half lengthwise, creating a folded edge running the width of the strip. Cut a 1-inch square from one of the teabag or patterned papers, focusing on a single image. Cut the remaining four teabag squares in half diagonally, making sure to cut each square in the same direction, leaving half the design on each triangle. With the white (unprinted) side of the paper facing up, fold the eight triangles into squares (figures 1–3).

5. **CONSTRUCT THE KALEIDOSCOPE:** Using a ruler and pencil, draw two diagonal lines from corner to corner on the work piece. Where the two lines intersect is the center. Glue the 1-inch teabag square onto the center of the work piece. Using either a template or ruler and pencil, draw a 3-inch square around the teabag square. Use this drawn square as a guide to make sure the strips of paper are placed parallel to its sides.

6. Place one of the lavender strips along the top edge of the teabag square and cut it slightly longer than the width of the square. Glue the strip in place with the folded edge overlapping the teabag square slightly (see section 1 on the pattern). As you layer the strips to form the kaleidoscope design, cut pieces as needed from one strip until it's too short to use, then begin cutting another strip.

7. Moving clockwise, place the remainder of the first strip against the right side of the teabag square and cut it long enough to cover both the right side of the square and the width of the previous strip. Glue it in place with the folded edge overlapping both the teabag square and the previously glued strip (see section 2). Next, place a lavender strip on the bottom of the teabag square and cut it long enough to cover the side of the square and the width of the previous strip. Glue as before (see section 3). To complete the first layer of the kaleidoscope design, place another lavender strip along the left side of the teabag square and cut it long enough to cover the left side of the square, the width of the previous strip, and the width of the first strip placed. Glue as before (see section 4). Make sure to use the drawn square as a guide to placing the strips on straight.

8. To add the second layer of the design, begin at the top of the square again and, moving clockwise, place the ivory pearl strips in the same manner as the lavender layer, making sure the new strips slightly overlap the previous ones, allowing ¼ inch of the lavender to show. Glue in place. Place one folded teabag square seam side down in each corner of the layered strips, covering both layers. Make sure the unfolded edges of the teabag squares are aligned with the unfolded edges of the paper strips. Glue in place.

9. Beginning at the top again, repeat a layer of the lavender strips, making sure to slightly overlap both the edges of the folded teabag squares in the corners and all but ¼ inch of the previous layer of strips. Add a final layer of ivory strips. This last layer of strips should completely cover the outline of the square drawn on the work piece. Glue the remaining four folded teabag squares in place in the corners, making sure they are covering the previously placed two layers of strips. Place the cutout frame over the work piece to make sure the ends of the papers are not showing through.

10. Tape the completed work piece to the back of the frame using transparent tape, making sure to center the kaleidoscope pattern so that the ends of the papers don't show through the frame.

11. Using the edging scissors, cut a decorative edge all around the base card. Center and mount the framed work piece (page 16) onto the front of the base card using double-sided tape.

VARIATION

Create a smaller kaleidoscope of this pattern by placing only two layers of strips of the same color. Use a complementary paper for both the folded corner squares and the center square.

Stitched Kaleidoscope

Replacing the strips of paper with layers of different colored metallic stitching makes an elegant alternative. The center square, corners of each layer, and printed background are all cut from the same sheet of origami paper.

YOU'LL NEED

PAPERS

Cardstock: gold pearl, black, black pearl (8½ x 11-inch sheets)

Black origami paper with gold Chinese characters (8½ x 11-inch sheet)

EMBELLISHMENTS

Metallic thread #4 braid: green, variegated gold/green, variegated gold/green/black

SUPPLIES

Template for ¾-inch square

Hand-sewing needle

Glue stick

Tapes: removable, transparent, double-sided

Scissors

Pencil

Paper cutter or craft knife and metal ruler

Craft foam (12 x 18-inch sheet)

Perforating tool

Scoring tool and bone paper folder (optional)

1. **CUT THE PAPERS:** From the gold pearl cardstock, cut a 3½-inch square for the work piece. From the black cardstock, cut a 4¼-inch square. From the black pearl cardstock, cut a rectangle 5¼ x 10½ inches for the base card. From the origami paper, cut a 5-inch square and, using the template, thirteen ¾-inch squares.

2. Score and fold the black pearl base card (page 16) in half to form a 5¼-inch square.

3. Following the instructions in Getting Started (page 13), transfer the embroidery pattern to the gold pearl work piece, making the necessary perforations. Glue one small origami square onto the center of the work piece, making sure not to cover any of the perforations.

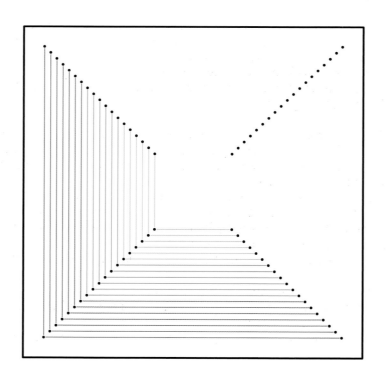

4. **EMBROIDER THE PATTERN:** With the pattern markings to guide you, stitch the three "layers" of the kaleidoscope design. Each layer comprises a square with six long straight stitches on a side, except the last layer, which has seven. Using the green metallic thread, stitch the centermost square (layer), completing one side before moving, clockwise, to the next. Using the green/gold metallic thread, stitch the next square in the same manner. Stitch the outermost square using the gold/green/black metallic thread as you did the others, but with seven long straight stitches per side.

5. **FOLD AND POSITION THE CORNER PIECES:** With the white (unprinted) side of the paper facing up, fold each of the remaining twelve origami squares in half diagonally to make triangles. Fold them as neatly as possible and trim any white that is showing. Place a dab of glue inside each fold and press the halves together to make sure the triangles lay flat.

6. Glue one triangle to each of the corners of the metallic green square (layer), using the right angle formed by the first stitches of the metallic gold/green square to align the corners. In a similar manner, glue four triangles to the corners of the second square, aligning the right angles of the triangles with the right angles formed by the first stitches of the metallic gold/green/black square. Glue the remaining four triangles to the corners of the gold/green/black square, aligning the right angles of the triangles with the right angle formed by the last stitches of the square.

7. Center and mount the completed work piece (page 16) onto the black cardstock square using double-sided tape. Similarly center and mount these layers onto the large origami square. To finish, center and mount all the layers onto the front of the base card using double-sided tape.

Night Music

Layers of small folded squares and triangles in a music print and solid silver merge artfully to form this starburst kaleidoscope. The pattern is displayed in a round frame embellished with embroidered and beaded music notes.

YOU'LL NEED

PAPERS

Cardstock: black and denim blue
  (8½ x 11-inch sheets)

Metallic silver gray-blue paper
  (8½ x 11-inch sheet)

Teabag folding papers with music
  motif or motif of choice
  (six 1½-inch squares)

Lightweight silver paper

EMBELLISHMENTS

Variegated blue/green metallic
  thread #4 braid

Blue metallic thread

Blue seed beads (12)

SUPPLIES

Template for 2-inch circle and
  cutting tool

Hand-sewing and beading needles

Tapes: removable, transparent,
  double-sided

Glue stick

Scissors

Pencil

Paper cutter or craft knife and
  metal ruler

Craft foam (12 x 18-inch sheet)

Perforating tool

Scoring tool and bone paper
  folder (optional)

1. **CUT THE PAPERS:** From the black cardstock, cut a 3-inch square for the work piece and a 4¾-inch square. From the denim blue cardstock, cut a rectangle 5¼ x 10½ inches for the base card. From the metallic silver gray-blue paper, cut a 5-inch square. From the silver paper, cut four 1½-inch squares.

2. Score and fold the denim blue base card (page 16) in half to form a 5¼-inch square.

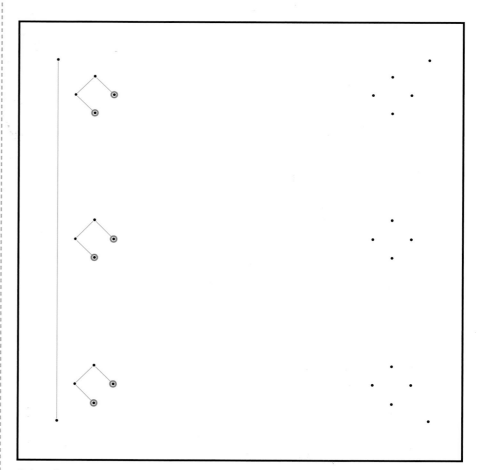

◉ **bead**

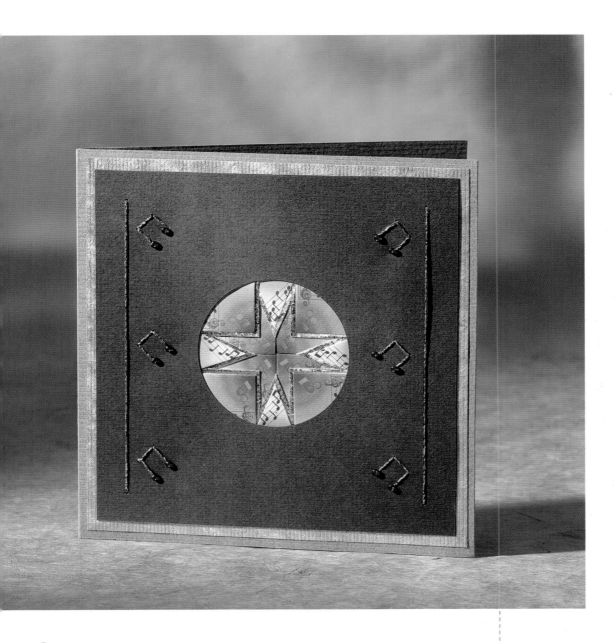

3. **MAKE THE FRAME:** Using the template and cutting tool, cut out a 2-inch circle from the center of the large black square to make the frame. The frame will be used later as a guide when making the kaleidoscope pattern.

4. **CUT AND FOLD THE TEABAG PAPERS:** Cut the six teabag squares in half diagonally, making sure to cut each square in the same direction so that half the design is on each triangle. Cut the four silver squares in half diagonally. Fold four silver triangles and eight teabag triangles

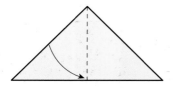

FIGURE 1

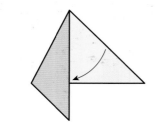

FIGURE 2

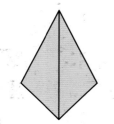

FIGURE 3

into squares (see Corner Square kaleidoscope, page 146, figures 1–3). Next, fold the remaining four teabag triangles and four silver triangles into kite shapes: With the white (unprinted) side of the paper facing up, fold each triangle in half. Open and fold the sides of each triangle downward from the point, so they are flush to the center crease. Make sure the sides do not overlap as you fold them to the center (figures 1–3).

5. **CONSTRUCT THE KALEIDOSCOPE:** Using a ruler and pencil, draw two diagonal lines from corner to corner on the work piece. Where the two lines intersect is the center. Using the template, draw a 2-inch circle around the center mark. To make the first layer of the kaleidoscope, glue four of the folded teabag squares to the center of the work piece. Make sure the folded edges of the squares face each other and the four points touch in the center (figure 4).

6. For the next layer, glue a silver kite seam side down, with its folded point on the line formed by two abutting teabag squares and ¼ inch from the center where all four squares meet. Similarly glue the other three silver kites onto the lines between the remaining three teabag squares (figure 5).

7. For layer three, glue a folded silver square in each corner on top of the four teabag squares and slightly overlapping the silver kites. Leave about ¼ inch between the right angle of each silver square and the center where the first four squares meet (figure 5).

8. For the last layer, glue one teabag kite over each silver kite, leaving ¹⁄₁₆ inch of the silver edge showing. Glue the remaining teabag squares over the silver squares in a similar manner (figure 6). This last layer should completely cover the outline of the circle drawn on the work piece. Place the cutout frame over the work piece to make sure the ends of the papers are not showing through.

9. **TRANSFER AND EMBROIDER THE STITCHING PATTERN:** Following the instructions in Getting Started (page 13), transfer the embroidery pattern to the cutout frame, making the necessary perforations. With the pattern markings to guide you and using the blue/green metallic thread, stitch each of the musical notes separately, carrying the thread between the notes on the back of the card. Make one long vertical stitch on the left and right sides of the card.

10. **SEW ON BEADS:** Following the instructions for adding beads (page 15), and using the blue metallic thread and beading needle, sew a blue seed bead onto the ends of each musical note.

11. Tape the completed work piece to the back of the stitched frame using transparent tape, making sure to center the kaleidoscope pattern so that the ends of the papers don't show through the frame.

12. Center and mount the framed work piece (page 16) onto the metallic silver gray-blue paper using double-sided tape. To finish, similarly center and mount these layers onto the front of the base card.

VARIATIONS

To make larger kaleidoscope designs of this pattern, use the same layering sequence but with larger teabag papers (2-inch squares) and contrasting squares. Cut the shape of a Christmas ornament or heart from a piece of cardstock to make a frame and tape it in place over the finished kaleidoscope design.

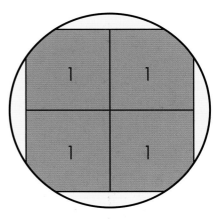

FIGURE 4

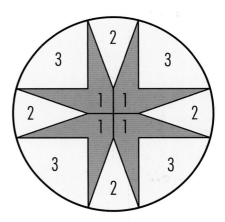

FIGURE 5

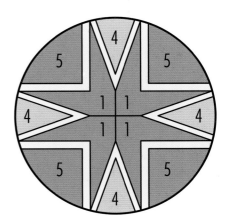

FIGURE 6

Crocus

This intricate-looking yet easy-to-make kaleidoscope uses teabag papers with only one design. The repeating patterns and colors result from the way the squares are cut and folded into kite-shaped pieces and placed in layers.

YOU'LL NEED

PAPERS

Cardstock: purple, green, ivory
(8½ x 11-inch sheets)

Metallic green paper
(four 1½-inch squares)

Teabag folding papers with
crocus pattern (eight 1½-inch
squares)

EMBELLISHMENT

Variegated green/gold/purple
thread #4 braid

SUPPLIES

Template for 2½-inch circle and
cutting tool

Corner punch

Hand-sewing needle

Glue stick

Tapes: removable, transparent,
double-sided

Scissors

Pencil

Paper cutter or craft knife
and metal ruler

Craft foam (12 x 18-inch sheet)

Perforating tool

Scoring tool and bone paper
folder (optional)

1. **CUT THE PAPERS:** From the purple cardstock, cut a 3½-inch square for the work piece and a 4¾-inch square. From the green cardstock, cut a 5-inch square. From the ivory cardstock, cut a rectangle 5¼ x 10½ inches for the base card. From the metallic green paper, cut four 1½-inch squares.

2. Score and fold the ivory base card (page 16) in half to form a 5¼-inch square.

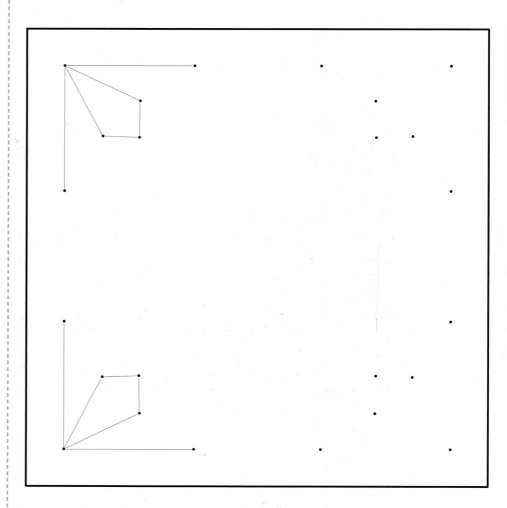

3. **MAKE THE FRAME:** Using the template and cutting tool, cut out a 2½-inch circle from the center of the large purple square to make the frame. This frame will be used later as a guide when making the kaleidoscope pattern.

4. **CUT AND FOLD THE TEABAG PAPERS:** Cut the eight teabag papers in half diagonally, making sure to cut each square in the same direction so that half the design is on each triangle. Cut the four metallic green squares in half diagonally. Fold all the triangles into a kite shape (see Night Music kaleidoscope, page 152, figures 1–3). Separate the teabag kites into two groups according to their designs.

5. **CONSTRUCT THE KALEIDOSCOPE:** Using a ruler and pencil, draw two diagonal lines from corner to corner on the work piece. Where the two lines intersect is the center. Using the template, draw a 2½-inch circle around the center mark. To make the first layer of the kaleidoscope design, place the long pointed end of eight folded teabag kites with the same design on the center mark of the work piece to form a complete circle. Adjust if necessary so that the points meet in the center and the sides abut (figure 1). Glue in place.

6. For the next layer, glue the long point of each of the remaining eight teabag kites on the line formed by two previously glued abutting kites and ¼ inch from the center where the points of the first layer meet (figure 2).

7. For the last layer, glue a green kite between each of the previously layered teabag kites, placing them about ½ inch back from the points of the previous layer (figure 3). This layer should completely cover the circle drawn on the work piece. Place the cutout frame over the work piece to make sure the ends of the papers are not showing through.

8. **TRANSFER AND EMBROIDER THE STITCHING PATTERN:** Following the instructions in Getting Started (page 13), transfer the embroidery pattern to the cutout purple frame, making the necessary perforations. With the pattern markings to guide you and using the variegated metallic thread, embroider each corner by stitching the kite shape first and then stitching out to both sides of the card. Work clockwise around the card, carrying the thread between corners on the back. When the stitching is complete, use the corner punch to cut decorative corners.

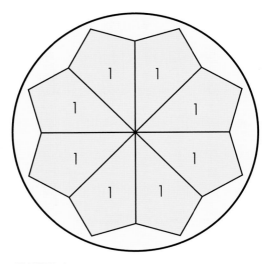

FIGURE 1

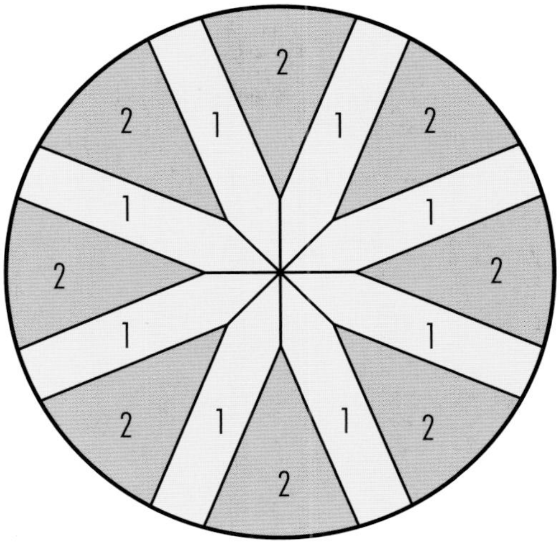

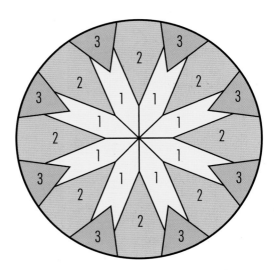

FIGURE 2

FIGURE 3

9. Tape the completed work piece to the back of the stitched frame using transparent tape, making sure to center the kaleidoscope pattern so that the ends of the papers don't show through the frame.

10. Center and mount the framed work piece (page 16) onto the green square using double-sided tape. To finish, similarly center and mount these layers onto the front of the base card.

ACKNOWLEDGMENTS

The following companies are acknowledged for their generous support:

Fiskars
305 84th Avenue South
Wasau, WI 54401
www.fiskars.com

Kreinik Thread
3106 Lord Baltimore Drive, Suite 101
Baltimore, MD 21244
www.kreinik.com

The Japanese Paper Place
77 Brock Avenue
Toronto, Ontario, Canada M6K 2L3
www.japanesepaperplace.com

Custom Paper Ltd.
5900 No. 2 Road, Unit 120
Richmond, B.C., Canada V7C 4R9
www.custompaper.ca

INDEX